James Bannister

A View of the Arts and Sciences

From the earliest times to the age of Alexander the Great

James Bannister

A View of the Arts and Sciences
From the earliest times to the age of Alexander the Great

ISBN/EAN: 9783337034511

Printed in Europe, USA, Canada, Australia, Japan

Cover: Foto ©ninafisch / pixelio.de

More available books at **www.hansebooks.com**

A

VIEW

OF THE

ARTS and SCIENCES,

FROM THE

EARLIEST TIMES

TO THE AGE OF

ALEXANDER the GREAT.

By the Rev. JAMES BANNISTER.

LONDON:

PRINTED FOR J. BELL, AT THE British-Library, STRAND,

MDCCLXXXV.

PREFACE.

THE diffusion of knowledge must be ever agreeable to the liberal and benevolent; and in an age like this, when a taste for reading universally prevails, an endeavour to recall the generality of readers from the perusal of frivolous publications (which, under the appellation of sentimental novels, enfeeble the mind, and render it susceptible of every evil impression) to the contemplation of those works of real genius, which, at the same time, refine

the

the taste, strengthen the understanding, and mend the heart, is an employment highly commendable. For the honour of our nation, it must be confessed, that the writings of ~~our~~ *the* most admired poets, historians, and orators of antiquity, have been translated into the English language, by men who knew how to preserve not only the sense, but the sprit of the great originals. Other writers, animated by the same laudable ambition, of communicating real knowledge, have explored the depths of antiquity, and explained the secrets of Philosophy and the Arts; subjects which have long engaged the attention of the author of the following dissertations, who, though conscious of the mediocrity of his talents, ventures to present his work to the public, encouraged by the

pleasing

pleasing expectation that it may give some persons, who have not enjoyed the advantage of a classical education, general ideas of the progress of the Arts and Sciences, and their connexion with morals and government; and excite others, whose genius is more active, to consult those fountains of true knowledge and sound philosophy, the ancient Greek and Roman writers. If either of these ends is attained, the author will think himself amply compensated for his trouble. It may not be improper in this place to inform the reader, that these dissertations were originally intended as part of a preliminary discourse to a translation of Aristotle's politics; a work the author was prevailed upon to undertake about two years ago, but having lately entered into a profession, the

duties

duties of which muſt neceſſarily engage a large portion of his time, he has for the preſent laid aſide all thoughts of proſecuting his tranſlation. To thoſe who may object, that many Arts and Sciences of the greateſt uſe and import-ance, are either wholly omitted, or but ſlightly touched upon, in the following diſſertations; the author begs leave to obſerve, that if favoured with the ap-probation of the public, it is his inten-tion to publiſh another volume, in which he will endeavour to ſupply every omiſſion and defect. Poetry was held in ſuch high eſteem in Greece, that many readers may be ſurpriſed that the author has not written a diſſertation on that ſubject. His excuſe is, that in his preface to a tranſlation of ſelect tragedies of Euripides, publiſhed in the year 1780, he had faid fo much on that fubject, that he thought he had nearly exhaufted it.

Devizes, Jan. 12, 1785.

A VIEW

A

V I E W

OF THE

ARTS and SCIENCES.

A R C H I T E C T U R E.

DENS and caves were the firſt habitations of
men; but the inconvenience and unwhole-
ſomeneſs of theſe gloomy manſions muſt have been
felt very early. Neither could the ſavage, depending on the fortune of the chace for his ſubſiſtence,
and conſequently obliged to lead a wandering life,
be always certain of meeting with theſe retreats
againſt the inclemency of the weather. The thick
ſhade of the foreſt might indeed ſerve to ſhelter
him from the fury of the ſtorm, but muſt certainly
prove inſufficient to protect him from the ill effects
of the mighty dews in warm, and the penetrating
powers of the froſt in cold climates.

A   Neceſſity,

Neceffity, which is the parent of every human invention, foon taught him to erect an habitation more fuitable to his wants. Houfes were built; at firft rude and imperfect, and compofed of the coarfeft materials, which varied with the foil and climate. In countries abounding with woods, branches of trees were thrown together inartificially, and covered with leaves, formed the firft dwellings; fuch are the wigwams ufed by the more favage tribes of Indians in North-America at this day. In warm climates (particularly in fome parts of Afia) the firft houfes were compofed of cane, or reed, which at the fame time that it fhaded them from the fcorching heat of the fun, by admitting the air, rendered their habitations pleafant and healthy. Thefe houfes were fituated on the extremity of the foreft, or on the banks of the river, for the convenience of hunting or fifhing, the only means of fubfiftence for man in the firft ftages of fociety.

Near the mouths of the Oronoque and Orellana (where the country is frequently overflowed to a vaft extent) the inhabitants build their houfes on trees. In countries where there is a fcarcity of wood, houfes, or rather tents, have been formed of fkins of beafts. Such I conceive to have been the firft habitations of the Arabs, which by being fo eafily portable, are admirably calculated for a country
where

where the want of pafture and water obliges them
fo frequently to change the place of their abode.

As long as mankind fubfifted by hunting and
fifhing we muft not expect to find any improvements made in Architecture. The time of a favage,
like his companion, the *wild beaft,* whom he too
much refembles, unlefs employed in the labours of
the chace, or in taking his neceffary repaft, is
either devoted to fleep, or at leaft to that fupine
indolence which falls little fhort of a total inactivity
of body and mind. To procure food, and guard
againft an immediate inconvenience, are the fole
objects of his care! Neither in the next ftage of
fociety, when men, grown more civilized, leave the
barbarous trade of the hunter for the more peace-
ful occupation of the fhepherd, can we hope to fee
Architecture flourifh. The fhepherd, for the convenience of pafture and water, is obliged to lead
a wandering life no lefs than the hunter. From
the account in Scripture of the Ifraelites during
the patriarchal ftate, it appears that they lived in
tents; the Tartars and wild Arabs know no other
habitation at this day, and affect to fpeak with
contempt of our nobleft pieces of architecture as a
weak attempt to rival the beauties of nature:
" What, fay they, are your fineft columns, com-
" pared with the ftately growth of a tree? or can
" your moft finifhed temples ftrike the mind with

" that

" that religious awe which it feels on entering a
" fhady and fequeftered grove?"

But when mankind, proceeding in their progrefs
towards civilization, apply themfelves to agriculture, new wants arife, and new arts are invented
to fatisfy thofe wants. The cultivator of the foil
foon difcovers that its productions are more than
fufficient for the fuftenance of himfelf and family—
he therefore difpofes of the fuperfluity, to procure
fome convenience, or to gratify fome vanity. From
hence proceeds the early divifion of mankind into
two claffes, the farmer and the artizan: the former receiving from the latter, in exchange for food,
the produce of his labour, which enables him to
enjoy, at firft the conveniencies, and afterwards
the luxuries of life. The hut, which gratified
every want of the hunter or fhepherd, is defpifed
by the farmer, as fmall and inconvenient. He
wifhes to erect a houfe more commodious and capacious; the artizan exhaufts all his ingenuity to
perfect this great work—but the advances in Architecture are at firft flow, as many fubfervient
arts muft be invented before it *can* arrive to any
great height. Trunks of trees, probably, were
made ufe of to fupport the roof—the walls were
formed of the branches covered with mud. This
led to new improvements; mankind fixed by the
introduction of agriculture to one fpot, thought of
ufing

uſing more durable materials in their buildings. Nature ſeems to have pointed out ſtone as the moſt obvious; particularly as we ſee in many countries a ſtriking ſimilitude between the projeƈtion of the rocks and ſome of our moſt admired buildings; but, notwithſtanding this, I am inclined to think brick was made uſe of in building long before ſtone. To dig ſtone from the quarry, afterwards to hew it and prepare it for building, cannot be done without the knowledge of many arts, and the inven- tion of many ingenious inſtruments. Brick, in ſome countries, particularly in Chaldea, was made with the greateſt eaſe—that Babylon was built with that material is allowed on all hands—in the moſt ancient hiſtory extant we find the Iſraelites, not employed in digging or hewing ſtone, but in making brick.

But without deciding poſitively on this queſtion, we may reaſonably ſuppoſe, that the trunks of trees, which formerly ſupported the roof, were ſuc- ceeded by pillars of ſtone or brick, and the walls compoſed of the ſame durable materials:—when I ſpeak of pillars, I muſt be underſtood to mean only the ſhaft—the baſe and capital were not in- vented till mankind had made great advances in civilization.

Devotion, which is ſo congenial to the human ſoul, that it accompanies the ſavage in the foreſt
(who

(who never fails to offer up his vows to the *good being* to give him fucceſs in the chace) is confiderably ſtrengthened by the introduction of agriculture. The aſſociation of men into villages, which is the immediate conſequence, tends to ſoften and humanize the heart; beſides, men who depend for ſubſiſtence on the annual production of their grain, ſee their hopes ſometimes blaſted by unfavourable ſeaſons; at other times, by a happy ſucceſſion of rain and ſunſhine, they find their labours crowned by an abundance which far exceeds their moſt ſanguine expectations. — This muſt naturally awaken in their breaſts ſentiments of gratitude and adoration, mixed with a fear of offending that deity who alone commands the ſeaſons. On the taking in of the harveſt, or the vintage, they offer to him the faireſt ſheaves of corn and the firſt cluſters of the vine, and invite him to partake in the general joy. Not content with this, they erect temples to his honour; and filled with the idea of the glorious inhabitant, exert the utmoſt efforts of human art and induſtry. To confirm this aſſertion, I have only to refer my readers to the account given by the Spaniards of the temple of the ſun in Peru, as well as the magnificent edifices devoted to the ſervice of religion in the ancient city of Mexico.

· Strength and convenience were, for a long time, the only objects confidered by men in their dwellings;

lings ; and the ornamental parts of Architecture were probably firſt uſed in their temples, and afterwards transferred to the palaces of their kings and great men, who owing their elevation of rank to their extraordinary virtues, were in ſome degree allied to the deity. .

It appears evident, from what has been ſaid above, that Architecture, properly ſo called, owes its riſe to agriculture; we muſt therefore trace its progreſs among thoſe nations which were the earlieſt civilized.

The Egyptians, not without reaſon, lay claim to this honour ; long before any profane hiſtories reach, even whilſt Jacob and his family led a paſtoral life; we find that nation governed by a regular police ; we ſee a king inveſted with all the external marks of dignity, and cities crowded with inhabitants.— Afterwards, when Jacob and his family, on the invitation of Joſeph, ſettled in Egypt, and their deſcendants were multiplied to a great people—the king, who dreaded their power, to divert their thoughts from any conſpiracy againſt his government, employed them as maſons and brickmakers, and ſeveral cities are ſaid to have been built by their hands: from hence it appears that the Egyptians, even at that early period, muſt have made confiderable advances·in Architecture. If we con-

ſult

fult profane hiftorians, we fhall find them unani-
mous in extolling the extent of the city of Thebes,
and the beauty and magnificence of its public and
private buildings. Homer, in the exaggerated
ftyle of poetry, fpeaks of twenty thoufand chariots
iffuing from its hundred gates. Diodorus Siculus
calls it the nobleft city in the world; admires its
ornamental works in gold, filver, and ivory; its
colloffal ftatues, and thofe immenfe obelifks,
formed of a fingle ftone, the remains of which
are yet beheld with admiration. The fame hiftorian defcribes the principal temple, which was to
be feen in his time, as of great extent; the walls
of wonderful thicknefs, and the decorations not
lefs admirable for their curious workmanfhip than
the richnefs of the materials; but the gold, filver,
ivory, and precious ftones, were pillaged by
Cambyfes in his invafion of that country, and
which afterwards ferved to adorn the palaces of
Perfepolis and Sufa;—but every thing I have hi-
therto mentioned falls infinitely fhort of the tomb
of Ofymandes, of which our hiftorian has given
a long defcription. It was built of ftones varioufly
coloured, and divided into many large apartments;
the greater part filled with coloffal ftatues of men
and beafts. In one part, the hiftory of the exploits
of Ofymandes was engraved on the walls; in another part, was feen an infinite number of ftatues
reprefenting an audience attentive to the decifions

of

of a full fenate—in the midſt ſtood the judge, at
his feet was placed the volume containing the laws
of Egypt, and round his neck was ſufpended, by a
ſtring, the image of Truth with her eyes ſhut : for
a more particular account of this wonderful building
I muſt refer the reader to Diodorus himſelf; and
ſhall only obſerve, that after making every allow-
ance for the exaggeration of vanity, and even
poetic fiction, enough remains to gives us an ex-
alted idea of the art and induſtry of the Egyptians.
Why ſhould I mention the pyramids, thoſe eternal
monuments of the oſtentation, vanity, and cruelty
of their kings, and the miſerable ſervitude of their
people, or enlarge on their immenſe obeliſks formed
of a ſingle ſtone, cut out of a rock in Upper-Egypt,
and from thence conveyed down their canals in
boats built for the purpoſe, and afterwards raiſed
to their perpendicular poſition by the united efforts
of myriads, employed in one common work ?

The Greeks derived their knowledge of Architecture from Egypt.—Cecrops and Danaus, with
their Egyptian colony, firſt prevailed on them to
leave their wandering life, to ſubmit to juſt and
equal laws, and to apply themſelves to agriculture
and the arts; but all that can be ſaid of the progreſs made by that nation, in Architecture, till the
time of the Trojan war, amounts to little more than
conjecture. We are informed that they lived in

B   cities,

cities, and erected temples for the worship of the gods, and palaces for the residence of their princes and great men.

Theseus, one of their most celebrated heroes, is said to have united the twelve cities of Attica under one government, and to have adorned the city of Athens with many noble buildings. For the state of Architecture, during the Trojan war, we must consult Homer; who, in the sixth book of his Iliad, gives us an account of the magnificent palace of Priam, containing apartments for his fifty sons and daughters, built entirely of marble, and raised on arches; from which we may infer, that the Greeks had already excelled their masters, the Egyptians, in Architecture; for it is remarkable, that that nation never knew how to turn an arch.

We have in the same author frequent descriptions of ornaments in gold, silver, brass, and ivory; and the imitative genius of man had already displayed itself in sculpture, painting, and statuary. Mention is likewise made of stately columns, but I can see nothing like a distinction of orders in building; consequently the account given by Vitruvius of the invention of the Ionic order, the honour of which he attributes to Ion, the son of Xuthus, must be rejected as fabulous, as well as the

the Doric order, which he affirms to have been invented by Dorus, a prince of Achaia.

The misfortunes of the princes engaged in the fiege of Troy, have proved a copious fubject for the epic and tragic mufe. We fee Ulyffes wandering for ten years through various climes, and driven on favage and inhofpitable coafts—Agamemnon murdered by his wife—Idomeneus and Diomede forced from their native foil, and obliged to feek fhelter in a foreign country; during this ftate of anarchy, confufion, and civil war, it is impoffible that the arts could flourish: but when the ftorm fubfided, and Oreftes was firmly eftablifhed on the throne of Argos, Mycenæ, and Sparta; during his long and happy reign, and that of his imme-diate fucceffor, Architecture, with the other arts, revived.

At length the Heraclidæ, eighty years after the deftruction of Troy, return into Peloponnefus—a long and cruel war fucceeds—the Pelopidæ are van-quifhed, and the Heraclidæ eftablifh themfelves in their ancient poffeffions; during this dreadful con-teft, learning, arts, and civility, feemed to breathe their laft. The old inhabitants, unable to bear the tyranny of their new mafters, emigrated in vaft numbers, and eftablifhing themfelves on the coaft of Afia-Minor, built the cities of Smyrna,

Halicarnaffus,

Halicarnaſſus, and Epheſus; here they had full
leiſure to cultivate the Arts and Sciences, which
they did with ſuch ſuccefs, that they boaſt the honour of giving birth to Homer, the father of poetry,
and Herodotus, the father of hiſtory. They likewiſe reduced Architecture to rules, and invented
the Doric and Ionic orders. The proportions are
taken from the human body, and as the height of
a man is ſix times the length of the foot, the height
of the pillar was, at firſt, equal to ſix times its
diameter; it was afterwards extended to ſeven
times. This pillar was adorned with a capital,
plain, and ſimple, and denoted ſtrength and ſoli-
dity; from the inventors, who were of Doric origin,
it derived its name. The Ionic pillar (invented
by the Ionians of Aſia-Minor ſome time afterwards)
repreſents a virgin in the bloom of youth—its proportions are more delicate, its capital is more or-
namented than the Doric, and its height is equal
to eight diameters. The characteriſtics of this
order are, chaſtity, neatnefs, and elegance, and
from the inventors it received its name. Theſe
improvements were ſoon conveyed from Aſia-
Minor to Greece. That country, already taught
to expreſs her ideas of ſtrength and elegance in her
buildings, wanted only juſt notions of the magnificent to render her knowledge of the art complete:
this was happily accompliſhed by the invention of
the Corinthian order; which, from the height of
the

the pillar, confifting of nine times its diameter, and the richnefs and variety of its ornaments, correfponded to every idea we could form of greatnefs.

We may reafonably fuppofe that the Greeks, poffeffed of thefe happy difcoveries, and aided by their natural genius, gave to Architecture its laft improvement; nor fhall we find ourfelves difap-pointed in our expectations. From the defcent of Xerxes to the death of Alexander the Great, we fee the elegant arts cultivated to that high degree as to leave fucceeding ages only the humble tafk of imitating what they could never equal.

Athens, which was burnt by the army of Xerxes, rofe from its afhes with new fplendour. The po-litical talents of Themiftocles, the juftice and integrity of Ariftides, the humanity of Cymon, the confummate prudence and admirable forefight of Pericles, which fucceffively held the reins of go-vernment, all tended to one point (viz.) that of making their country glorious and their people happy. Enriched by the fpoils of their vanquifhed enemies, and yet more by their extenfive commerce, liberality, tafte, and induftry were univerfally diffufed. Cymon, by his refined, elegant, and ge-nerous ftyle of living, contributed no lefs to adorn the city by works of art than to improve the manners

of

of its inhabitants. Pericles, by the number and magnificence of his public buildings, acquired the glorious appellation of fecond founder of Athens; the fame grandeur and elevation of thought, chaftifed by the fevereft judgment, which animated his orations, appeared in his ftatues and temples.

In the temple of Jupiter Olympius we fee form and colour given to the fublime conceptions of Homer in the ftatue of Jupiter, the work of the immortal Phidias. The foundations of this temple are faid to have been laid by Pififtratus, but I imagine all that was built of it before the expedition of Xerxes, muft have perifhed in the great conflagration which confumed the city—but the Athenians foon began to rebuild it, and adorned by the fucceffive labours and ingenuity of many generations, when finifhed, it exhibited an object more glorious than any which Egypt or Babylon had ever feen in the days of their greateft profperity and fplendour—in magnitude nearly equal to fome of their moft celebrated edifices; in chaftity of defign, in juftnefs of proportion, and in every thing that conftitutes true beauty, far fuperior. To defcribe the numerous porticos, temples, aqueducts, and the other monuments of ingenuity and tafte, with which this city abounded, does not fall in with the defign of my work; but the theatre is too extraordinary not to merit a particular account. It was

built

built of coftly marble, and fo large, that it was capable of holding thirty thoufand fpectators; circular on one fide, and fquare on the other; round the whole were ranges of porticos, according to the number of ftories, raifed one above the other. This building was open at the top; the reafon of which I conceive to be this: as the plays were acted in the day-time, the light of the fun might in fome meafure be neceffary for the actors; befides, it gave an air of probability to the drama, and made the reprefentation appear like a real action, which was a principal object with all their tragedians. But nothing in the Greek theatre ftrikes us with that aftonifhment, as the echea, or brazen veffels, as Vitruvius calls them, which were placed under the feats of the fpectators, and difpofed by the moft exact geometric and harmonic proportion, in fuch a manner as to reverberate the voice of the actor, and render the articulation more clear and harmonious; and fuch was the excellence of this contrivance, that a perfon placed in the furtheft part of the theatre could hear diftinctly every fyllable of the play. How this was accomplifhed is not eafy to conceive—certain I am, that it could not be effected without a more perfect knowledge, not only of Architecture, but of various branches of the mathematics, than we at prefent poffefs; for few of the advocates for the moderns will, I believe, have the vanity to affert, that any perfon of this

age

age can communicate found, clearly and diftinctly, by an invention of that nature, through the fmaller and lefs crouded theatres of London and Paris.

Let us now confider the comparative merits of the Egyptian and Grecian Architecture. On viewing the former, we are ftruck with that idea of grandeur which rifes from the magnitude of the object, and cannot help expreffing our admiration and aftonifhment, when we confider the vaft difproportion between the building and the builder! when we reflect on the limited powers of man, and behold the effects of united and continued labour. Their coloffal ftatues, and the laborious and minute ornaments, with which they overcharged their buildings, muft likewife excite in us an admiration of their induftry. But they were ftrangers to that beauty which proceeds from correctnefs of defign, and a graceful and harmonious difpofition of parts. They were likewife ignorant of what we confider as fome of the firft principles of Architecture. I have already obferved, that they knew not how to turn an arch, neither were they happy in the difpofition of their lights. Pillars, it is true, are to be feen in their buildings, but fo much out of all proportion, that inftead of a beauty, they may be confidered as a defect—the ornaments of the capital are laboured, lifelefs, and uniform. Egypt, though the parent of almoft every art, yet

never

never carried *one* to its higheſt ſtate of poſſible perfection.   The fire of genius was extinguiſhed by the rigid laws, and ſtrict œconomy, of their government; but in Greece the powers of the human mind had full liberty to expand themſelves, and to that happy climate we owe that combination of judgment and feeling which conſtitutes true taſte.   This reigns in all their works of art, and whether we contemplate a building or a ſtatue, we are ſtruck with an idea of beauty, the effect of a juſt imitation of nature, or a conformity between the object before us, and the deſign of the artiſt; if, deſcending to particulars, we examine a ſingle column, we ſhall find it perfect in all its parts; and that the length of the ſhaft, and the ornaments of its capital, are ſo formed as to convey ideas of ſtrength, elegance, or grandeur, the characteriſtics of the three orders, and which include every modification of either utility or beauty.

From what has been ſaid, I think I may venture to affirm, that Architecture in Greece, during the time of Alexander the Great, had reached the higheſt perfection of which it is capable.   That the Greeks were far ſuperior, in that art, to the Egyptians, Babylonians, and all the nations of antiquity; and that the excellence of the moderns conſiſts in a happy imitation of thoſe models of perfection which are left us by that polite and enlightened people.

C   A S T R O.

ASTRONOMY.

IF we carry back our views to the remoteft antiquity, and contemplate *man* in the earlieft
ftages of fociety; we fhall find him ftruck with the
appearance of the heavenly bodies. The regular
fucceffion of day and night gives him the firft idea
of the divifion of time, and the fun and moon will
be the firft objefts of his attention. The fplendour
of the former moving in an unclouded fky—the
more fober majefty of the latter, accompanied by
an innumerable hoft of ftars, muft fill him with
aftonifhment and admiration; but when he difcovers their benign influence on the fruits of the
earth, on animals, and on man, or that the fun (to
ufe the fublime expreffion of the Peruvians) is the
foul of the univerfe, which animates every part, he
will be naturally led to regard that glorious luminary with fentiments of gratitude and adoration.
The moon, as next in dignity, will likewife be
confidered as an objeft of worfhip.

Thus we find that all nations, however they differ in language, climate, and manners, have agreed
in ranking the fun and moon among their firft
deities, till a more abftrafted philofophy taught

them to confider thefe luminaries, fo wonderful in their powers and beneficial in their influence, only as the emanation of that Divine Mind which ex- ifled from all eternity.

The different phafes of the moon muft very early have engaged the attention of mankind; and it could not be long before they difcovered that fhe run through all her changes and completed one revolution in twenty-nine days and a half. This formed the fecond divifion of time;—and whilft men led a wandering life, fubfifting on the fponta- neous fruits of the earth, or by hunting and fifhing, no other divifion was neceffary. Thus the inhabi- tants of the interior parts of Africa, and many nations of favages in North and South America, at this day, have no other method of reckoning time but by moons. But when men applied themfelves to Agriculture, it was neceffary for them to extend their views further, to mark the feafons and afcer- tain the proper time for fowing and reaping their grain; this could not be done accurately without fixing the term of a revolution of the fun; a work of no fmall difficulty, and far beyond the powers of the human mind juft emerging from a ftate of barbarifm. But they obferved, that after twelve revolutions of the moon, they faw a return of the fame feafons, and from thence concluded that one folar, was equal to twelve lunar revolutions;

the

the firſt year muſt therefore conſiſt of three hundred
and fifty-four days, that is, eleven days, ſix hours,
and forty-nine minutes leſs than the true ſolar year.
The defeĉt of this reckoning muſt very ſoon have
been felt, as in ſeventeen years the courſe of the
ſeaſons would be inverted.   To remedy this,
they made the months conſiſt of thirty days, twelve
of which formed a year of three hundred and ſixty
days, from whence came the diviſion of the ecliptic
into three hundred and ſixty degrees. This luni-
ſolar year was in uſe among the Aſſyrians, Babylonians, Iſraelites, and all the civilized nations of
Aſia; it was likewiſe adopted by the Greeks and
Latins, and even by the Egyptians till the reign of
Ammon, which ſir Iſaac Newton places one thou-
ſand and thirty-four years before the Chriſtian æra.
The Egyptians, ſays Diodorus Siculus, reckon
their days, not by the courſe of the moon, but by
the courſe of the ſun; their year conſiſts of twelve
months of thirty days, to which they add five days
and ſix hours, which completes the ſolar revolution.
They uſe no intercalation, like the Greeks; and
as their calendar is more correĉt, their calculations
of ſolar and lunar eclipſes are more to be depended
on than thoſe of any other nation.

    In memory of this moſt wonderful diſcovery,
the ſame author relates, that in the tomb of Oſy-
mandes they placed a golden circle, one cubit in
thickneſs

thicknefs and three hundred and fixty-five in compafs. This circle was divided into three hundred
and fixty-five equal parts, which correfponded to
the days of the year, on which the heliacal rifings
and fettings of the ftars were marked. This circle,
together with other valuable monuments of Egyptian learning and ingenuity, was deftroyed by
Cambyfes in his cruel invafion of that country.
From the teftimony of this, as well as every other
ancient writer, it appears that the Egyptians applied themfelves very early to the ftudy of Aftronomy, and were celebrated for their fuperior knowledge in that fcience above all nations.

The ferenity of their fky, feldom obfcured by
clouds, enabled them to contemplate the heavenly
bodies in all their glory. · The fertility of their foil,
which afforded fubfiftence without much labour,
induced a confiderable part of the fociety to devote
themfelves to a life of ftudy and contemplation;
and above all, the periodical overflowing of the
Nile rendered them particularly attentive in marking
the feafons—for this annual inundation covered all
the low lands of Egypt, and obliged the inhabitants
to build their towns and villages on eminences, and
fecure them againft the rifing waters by large and
deep ditches; a work of incredible labour. Not to
mention thofe famous canals, which, breaking the
force of the torrent, conveyed the waters through
a thoufand

a thoufand different channels, and diffufed fertility
over the whole country. Thus did the induftry and
ingenuity of the Egyptians convert into a bleffing,
what feemed intended by nature as a curfe. Diodorus Siculus relates, that in the reign of their
ancient kings, high towers were erected, on which
perfons were placed to mark accurately from day
to day the augmentation and diminution of the
river. Thefe annual obfervations were preferved
with great care: from a due attention to which
the Egyptians houfed their cattle, retired from the
country into the towns, and forefeeing the inundation, expected it with great tranquillity.

The Greeks derived their knowledge of Aftronomy, as of almoft every other fcience, from Egypt.
Their year confifted, as I before obferved, of
three hundred and fixty days, which, though more
perfect than the lunar year of three hundred and
fifty-four days, yet as it was five days, fix hours,
and forty-nine minutes fhort of the true folar year,
muft be confidered as very defective, as in the
courfe of a little more than thirty-four years, by
this reckoning, the order of the feafons muft be
inverted. To remedy this inconvenience, they
corrected their months and years by the revolution
of the fun and moon, omitting a day or two in a
month as often as they found the month exceed
the revolution of the moon; and adding a month
                                                    to

to the year as often as they found the twelve lunar
months too short for the return of the four seasons.
To the twelve lunar months the Greeks added an
intercalary month every other year, which they
called Dieteris; and finding the year too long, in
the course of eight years, by a month, they omitted
every eighth year an intercalary month, which they
called Octæteris. This method of intercalation is
said to have been introduced by· Cadmus, who
brought it from Phœnicia; but during the times of
the Persian empire, the Greek astronomers changed
their manner of intercalating the three months in
the Octæteris. From their ignorance of the true
solar revolution, the calendar of the Greeks must
be subject to continual variation. The first month
of their luni-solar year must begin sometimes before and sometimes after the vernal equinox, by
reason of the intercalary month; and the ancient
astronomers were divided in opinion about fixing
the equinoctial point. The difficulty was increased
by the precession of the equinoxes, of which they
were ignorant. Meton and Euctemon reformed
the Greek calendar in the year before Christ 432,
by their famous lunar cycle of nineteen years. To
nineteen lunar years they added seven intercalary
months; this cycle, though it does not correspond
exactly with nineteen solar revolutions, yet is freer
from error than any that was formed before. The
Chaldeans, who were much addicted to the study

of

of Aftronomy (and who were the inventors of judicial Aftrology) in the year 884 before Chrift, adopted the Egyptian year of three hundred and fixty-five days, and commenced at that period their famous æra of Nabonaffar.

It is probable that the Egyptians difcovered the true length of the folar year by meafuring the meridional fhadow of the fun; they ufed at firft natural gnomons, fuch as mountains and trees, which fuggefted the idea of artificial, and we have reafon to imagine, that their famous obelifks were erected for aftronomical purpofes, and not merely for an oftentatious difplay of the wealth of their kings.

From the imperfect ftate of the Greek calendar, many refpectable writers have imagined that the Greeks, captivated by the charms of eloquence, poetry, and thofe elegant arts which are the children of fancy, paid little attention to Aftronomy; but fir Ifaac Newton, whofe authority on this fubject ought to have great weight, affirms that Chiron formed a fphere for the princes who engaged in the Argonautic expedition, and fixed the equinoctial and folftitial points. The names of the conftellations infcribed on this fphere, as the fame admirable philofopher obferves, relate to the Argonauts and their cotemporaries, and to perfons one or two generations older. It at firft appears difficult

3   to

to conceive that the Greeks, at fo early a period, fhould have made fuch great advances in Aftronomy; but we ought to confider that the multitude of ftars which are fcattered over the face of heaven, engaged the attention of mankind almoft as early as the fun and moon, firft from curiofity; afterwards their utility was difcovered, though partially, by the moft favage nations, who in travelling through their deferts have no other guide but the ftars to direct them. This neceffarily induced them to fix their attention to thofe ftars, which from their fplendour, and above all, their pofition in the heavens, were beft calculated for that purpofe. Thus the Iriquois, before the arrival of the Europeans, were acquainted with the polar ftar, and the conftellation of the Great-Bear. The Greenlanders know the polar ftar, the great and leffer bear. Seadogs make a confiderable part of their fubfiftence. Thofe amphibious animals are not to be caught except at night; the appearance of the ftars, therefore, is a fignal for the Greenlanders to hunt the fea-dogs, and the name they give the Urfa Minor is expreffive of the action of hunting. The inhabitants of North-America are not ignorant of the Pleiades, Hyadaes, and Orion, and, according to Condamine, they call the galaxy, or milky-way, the road of fouls. It appears extraordinary that they fhould diftinguifh their conftellations in the earlieft times by the names of men and animals,

D   and

and that in fome inftances the names fhould corre-
fpond with thofe adopted by the Greeks: thus the
conftellation of the Great-Bear, is called by the fame
name in North-America, as in Europe; not from
any fimilitude of the conftellation to that animal,
but becaufe a bear is the moft remarkable animal
which inhabits the Northern regions.   In Egypt
and Chaldea, the fame conftellation is defigned by
the fymbol of the Chariot, to which it bears fome
refemblance.   The inhabitants of thofe countries
had not, when the fphere was formed, extended
their voyages fo far, as to difcover that the bear
is a native of the North.   The Chaldeans, Ara-
bians, Perfians, and Greeks, have reprefented Orion
by the emblem of a giant; this conformity is attributed to the large fpace that conftellation occupies
in the heavens.

From what has been faid, it is evident, that the
aftronomical knowledge of thofe people we term
barbarous and uncivilized, is greater than our pride
is ready to allow.   Accuftomed from our infancy to
attend to eftablifhed forms, and early taught to think
by rule, we feldom contemplate objeɛts but through
the medium of learning, and cannot eafily form a
conception of the bold operations of the human
mind, left to itfelf, and perufing with an unpreju-
diced eye the great volume of nature.—The Phœnicians have the honour of being the firft people

who applied the knowledge of the stars to the purpofes of navigation, and reduced commerce to a
fcience. They fent colonies to Africa and Spain, commanded the whole trade of the Mediterranean-Sea,
and extended their voyages even to Britain, as early,
or probably earlier than any profane hiftories reach.
That it was impoffible to complete the long voyages
of the Phœnicians, without a knowledge of the conftellations, and accurate obfervations on the rifing
and fetting of the ftars, no perfon will be fo hardy as
to deny.

It is well known that Cadmus and his colony of
Phœnicians introduced letters, mufic, poetry, the fa-
brication of metals, and practical Aftronomy, into
Greece, above one hundred years before the Argonautic expedition. That the Greeks received
from them a knowledge of thofe conftellations
which Chiron is faid to have infcribed in his fphere,
is very probable; not that I pretend to affirm, that
the conftellations were called by the fame name in
Phœnicia as in Greece. Chiron, to gratify the vanity of his countrymen, immortalized their heroes
by giving their names to many of the conftellations:
but the arrangement of the ftars, I fhould fuppofe,
though reprefented by different fymbols, was nearly
the fame in both countries. But without infifting
too much on thefe arguments, it is not eafy to conceive how the Argonauts could perform their long

D 2 and

and dangerous voyage to Colchis, at the extremity of the Euxine-Sea, without a knowledge of the greater part of the conftellations faid to have been marked on the fphere of Chiron. In the fame fphere, we are told, that the equinoĉtial and folftitial points were fixed; but this could not be done with any great accuracy, as the Greeks were at that time unacquainted with the preceffion of the equinoxes. —From the Argonautic expedition, to the time of Thales the Milefian, we have no account of the Greek Aftronomy. That great philofopher wrote a book on the tropics and equinoxes, and prediĉted an eclipfe of the fun, as appears by the teftimony of Herodotus.—To give a particular account of the tenets of Thales, and his fucceffors of the Ionic fchool, in this place, would be improper. Let it fuffice to obferve, that almoft every philofopher adopted a favourite fyftem, which he conceived himfelf bound in honour to defend. Thus thofe ta-lents which ought to have been employed in the calm inveftigation of truth, ferved only to perpetuate difputes, and involve the cleareft perceptions of the human mind in doubt and uncertainty. Amid this confufion of fyftems, Socrates appeared in the world;—poffeffed of a genius comprehenfive and fublime,—a judgment acute and penetrating,—and a temper modeft and amiable,—attentive only to the caufe of truth and virtue, this great man rejeĉted all the fyftems of natural philofophy which prevailed

in

in his time, as idle and unfatisfactory, and devoted himfelf entirely to the ftudy and practice of moral philofophy ;——his difciple Plato, though he retained the doctrines and important truths inculcated by his great mafter, yet did not reject the aid of natural philofophy : from a contemplation of the heavenly bodies, he drew a parallel between the regularity of their motions, and the beauty and harmony of virtue ; and endeavoured, by raifing the thoughts of his followers above the objects of fenfe, to infpire them with juft notions of the Deity, and to animate them to the practice of thofe virtues which exalt and dignify human nature.

Pythagoras, who flourifhed in Italy about the fixtieth olympiad, is reported to have given a true account of the planetary motions, and to have formed that fyftem of the univerfe, which was afterwards revived by Copernicus in the fifteenth century. This fyftem is not fuppofed to have been the invention of Pythagoras, but tranfplanted by that philofopher from Egypt to Italy ; for it is agreed that he fpent twenty-two years in the Eaft, and that nothing might retard him in his purfuit of knowledge, he fcrupled not to fubmit to the cuftoms moft peculiar to thofe nations. But his aftronomical difcoveries did not meet with the fuccefs they deferved. Ariftotle rejected his fyftem : but it appears that that philofopher had but a confufed notion of

the

the doctrines of Pythagoras; for the warmeſt admirers of Ariſtotle muſt confeſs, that his penetrating genius, which enabled him to perform wonders in his ethics, logic, phyſics, and metaphyſics, has failed him in his aſtronomical inquiries; not that I deny but even in that ſcience his reaſonings are acute and ſubtle, but many of his concluſions are overturned by modern diſcoveries.

From what has been ſaid, it appears that the Greeks, in the time of Alexander the Great, were inferior to their maſters the Egyptians in Aſtronomy; it is impoſſible to affirm with certainty, whether they were equal to the Chaldeans and Phœnicians in that ſcience, but I ſhould rather judge them to be inferior. For the honour of the moderns it muſt be acknowledged, that the ancients at no period ever equalled the laſt and the preſent age in aſtronomical knowledge. We are indebted for this ſuperiority in ſome meaſure to the diſcovery of the mariner's compaſs, which has enabled us to extend our navigation to the moſt remote countries; to the many ingenious inſtruments we poſſeſs, which were unknown to the ancients; and above all, to our optical glaſſes, which extending the bounds of human viſion, have opened to our view an infinite number of new worlds, in the contemplation of which the moſt enlarged mind is loſt in aſtoniſhment and admiration.

LANGUAGE.

L A N G U A G E.

ROUSSEAU fuppofes that men lived many ages
without the ufe of language. It will be needlefs to expofe the abfurdity of this opinion, and a
mere wafte of words to give a ferious anfwer to a
wild vifionary, whofe writings are no lefs contradictory to common fenfe, than fubverfive of every
principle of morality and religion. But it muft be
confeffed that the firft efforts towards language are
very feeble, and confift of little more than inarticulate cries, expreffive of aftonifhment, fear, terror,
and fome of the ftrongeft emotions of the human
foul. Thefe cries are few in number, and inadequate to the neceffities of mankind, even in their
moft favage ftate. They muft therefore have learnt,
in the earlieft times, to vary and enlarge thefe
founds by articulation; for which the organs of
man are wonderfully adapted. From lengthened
founds thus divided, which is the peculiar province
of articulation, the firft language was formed; but we
muft not expect to find in it any thing like the
parts of fpeech: not only the verb, but even the
noun is wanting in the moft barbarous languages.
The reafon I conceive to be this: it is impoffible to

give

give a name to an object without a diſtinct idea. All ideas are formed by abſtraction and combination; operations of the mind to which an uncultivated ſavage is a ſtranger, for external objects ſtrike his ſenſes, not in their ſimple, but in their mixed and compounded ſtate, and may be conſidered as a combination of qualities united in one ſubſtance. To ſeparate the qualities from the ſubject, and to diſtinguiſh thoſe which are peculiar to it, as an individual, from thoſe which are general to it, as a ſpecies, requires much thought and reflection; yet without this no regular language can be formed.

In the Huron language we ſee a ſentence frequently expreſſed by a ſingle word, and the action, agent, and ſubject, ſtrangely mixed together. Except in a very few inſtances, they have no term for a ſubſtance unconnected with its qualities. Conſequently the words in this language expreſs not only every object, and every action, but all their various relations as ſo many ſeparate individuals; and it has been obſerved, that whatever analogy their words may have in ſignification, they have none in ſound. This is ſo remarkable, that to expreſs the addition of a negation, or even a change of perſons, they make uſe of a word entirely new. From whence can this imperfection in the art of ſpeech ariſe, but from the confuſed impreſſions made on the mind of man by external objects which he has never
arranged

ranged under diftinct and general heads, or feparated from thofe circumftances which attended
them when they firft ftruck his fenfes? If I may
be allowed to carry back my views to thofe remote
times where human reafon affords but a fcanty light,
and too often refigns her place to hypothefis and conjecture, I fhould imagine that the firft impreffions a
folitary favage muft feel, would be thofe of aftonifhment and terror. Thefe would gradually diminifh
as he became more familiarized to thofe objects which
at firft from their novelty appeared terrible; he
would then endeavour to provide for the necessities
of nature, and like other gregarious animals, affo-
ciate with his own fpecies; an union of fexes would
take place, and political bodies would be formed on
the principle of mutual defence. In this progreffive ftate towards what may be called the firft rudi-
ments of fociety, the faculties of favages muft gradually unfold themfelves. I have already obferved,
that in the Huron language we frequently fee the action, agent, and fubject, ftrangely mixed together,
and expreffed by a fingle word. This I fuppofe to
have prevailed univerfally in the firft formation of
that Language; but at prefent, in fome cafes, we fee
the fubject feparated from the action: this fhews
that they have at leaft made fome improvement. In
the Caribbee language they have gone yet further;
and in thofe objects with which they are moft con-
verfant, fuch as mountains, rivers, trees, &c. have

E   fepa-

feparated the fubftance from the quality, and have
even diftinguifhed them by a general name. As
they grow more civilized, the number of thefe
general terms muft increafe, and regular nouns will
be formed.   They will next afpire to greater improvements, and, by feparating the action from the
agent, form that moft artificial part of fpeech the
verb, and this they have in fome inftances already
done; but the variations of time and perfon in their
verbs, and the relations in their nouns, are marked
by tones, of which in all the barbarous languages
they have a great variety. This gives a kind of
chaunting cadence to their Language, from which
circumftance fome modern philofophers have fuppofed that the firft founds of man were imitative of
the notes of birds. Derivation, compofition, and
inflexion, by which alone the moods and tenfes in
verbs, and the cafes in nouns are formed, muft be
confidered as one of the refinements of Language,
and the work of more enlightened ages.

To fum up what I have faid in as few words as
poffible; the progreffion of Language I conceive to
be nearly as follows :
   Firft.   Inarticulate founds.
   Secondly. Confufed perceptions mixed and expreffed by a fingle word.
   Thirdly. Subftances abftracted from their qualities,
which form nouns.
                                 Fourthly.

Fourthly. The actions feparated from the agents, which form verbs.

Fifthly. Derivation, and compofition.

Abftract nouns, derived from adjectives, fuch as flight, whitenefs, temperance; and thofe more artificial fubftances, fuch as motion, colour, virtue, &c. are not to be met with in any of the barbarous languages. The favages are unacquainted with fyntax, for they have no prepofitions or conjunctions. In their difcourfe, as we may obferve in children, when they firft learn to fpeak, they ufe words unconnected with one another. To make themfelves underftood, it is therefore neceffary that they fhould affume a variety of tones and geftures. This is fo obfervable in all the North-American tribes, that they have been called by fome of our countrymen a nation of orators. Words of an immeafurable length are likewife peculiar to the barbarous languages, of which Condamine has given a famous example in the word Poetazzarorincouroac, which fignifies three. This peculiarity, I conceive, took its rife from their cuftom of expreffing feveral ideas by one word. Though fome philofophers fuppofe it to be nothing but the remains of their original inarticulate cries. The Language of the favages is energetic, becaufe their ideas are copied immediately from nature; it is concife, becaufe they have more ideas than terms, and from the fame

E 2   caufe

cauſe it is figurative. A ſavage finding himſelf at a loſs how to expreſs an abſtract idea, has recourſe to material images, and fixes on one that bears ſome analogy to the conception formed in his mind, by means of which he explains his meaning, and thus makes uſe of the metaphor. This beautiful figure, which is the ſoul of rhetoric and poetry, ſprung firſt from the poverty of that Language which it was afterwards deſtined to beautify and adorn. As clothes, to uſe the words of Tully, were firſt worn from neceſſity, afterwards for ornament. The hyperbole is a figure in rhetoric the ſavages are very fond of. This is the effect of that aſtoniſhment on beholding a new object which is the concomitant of ignorance. Many of our countrymen who have lived among the ſavages, ſtruck with their frequent or rather conſtant uſe of rhetorical figures, have aſcribed to them a great warmth and vigour of imagination, and ſuppoſed, that their Language, of all others, was the beſt fitted for poetry. To deny that it abounds with many bold and animated expreſſions, would be unjuſt; and on ſome occaſions we meet with an aſtoniſhing elevation of thought: but if it is the chief object of poetry to lay open the inward paſſions and affections of mankind, and to form the mind to virtue by example; we muſt certainly ſeek for that divine ſcience among people more civilized. Not to mention that the obſcurity and want of pre-
ciſion

cifion fo obfervable in their Language, renders it unfit even for defcription.

From what has been faid, it appears that the Language of a favage is in a progreffive ftate, but the improvements muft be very flow, owing to the limited fphere in which he moves. But let us fuppofe a Magno Capac to arife in the defert, endowed with fuperior talents, and animated by the godlike ambition of making his fellow-creatures happy. The wandering tribes, inftructed by him in agriculture and the arts, will leave the forefts, and form fixed habitations in villages and towns: they will exchange a precarious for a certain fubfiftence: that quick tranfition from fupine indolence, to the moft fatiguing labour, which marks the life of a favage, will be fucceeded by regular induftry; the domeftic relations will be more accurately afcertained; the warm and focial affections, by frequent converfe, enlarged and improved; the finer feelings awakened, and thofe fublime virtues excited, which form the patriot and hero. From this happy change, new objects muft arife every day; the fphere of man's ideas will be enlarged, and the improvements in Language proportionably rapid. From their multiplicity, it will foon be found impoffible to invent a new word for every new idea; this will lead men to arrange them under general heads. From individuals they will afcend to the fpecies, from the

fpecies

species to the genus. This gives rise to derivation
and composition, which by preserving that analogy
between words, which is to be found in their cor-
respondent ideas, not only render Language more
accurate and precise, but facilitate the progress of
the human mind in science. We find this exemplified in the Greek language, which is of all others
the most derivative; where almost every substance
contains a definition, when resolved into its elementary parts. Reasoning yet more abstractedly, they will
discover that every thing in nature, has either a se-
parate and independent existence, or else it exists
only as the energy or affection of something else; the
former of these may be termed a substance, the other
an attribute; and under these two classes all our ideas
may be arranged. Attributes are subdivided into those
which have the power of assertion, which constitute
what we call verbs, and those which simply denote
quantities and qualities, which are termed adjectives;
substances are expressed by nouns. Besides these
terms, there are others in the refinement of Language,
significant only by relation; such are articles and
conjunctions; the other parts of speech, such as
pronouns, adverbs, &c. I conceive are included within some of the species above mentioned. Let us now
suppose a Language formed, regular and copious,
abounding in words not only proper for the ordinary
occurrences of life, but expressive of the operations
of the mind. We will suppose considerable advances

to

to have been made in morality and legiſlation; the baſis of which are abſtraƈt ideas : yet this Language, which is only a modification of found, is limited by ſpace and duration; ſomething is yet wanting to render it complete; the happy art of communicating our thoughts at a diſtance, and giving a viſible form to our ideas. An art ſo neceſſary to man as a ſocial, and yet more as a political animal! The moſt natural and obvious method of recording conceptions, ſeems to be painting the images of things ; of which we have a memorable example on the arrival of the Spaniards in the kingdom of Mexico. The natives, ſtruck with the ſingularity of their appearance, difpatched to their king Montezuma, a large cloth covered with an infinite number of figures, repreſenting the Spaniards and their ſhips. Even the North-American ſavages have a method of perpetuating a viƈtory, by engraving on a tree the contending parties, diſtinguiſhed by the badges of their tribes; and the number of ſlain are marked by figures of men without heads. The inconvenience attending this mode of communication, muſt have been very ſoon felt. To give a ſeparate form to every individual, muſt have been an endleſs labour, and the bulk of their volumes conſequently immenſe. This induced the more ingenious to contrive a method of abridging their charaƈters, and gave riſe to hieroglyphics, an improvement of all others the moſt celebrated, and in which the Egyptians particularly

3   excelled,

excelled. The firft and moft fimple method of a-bridgment, was to make the principal circumftance in an action ftand for the whole: thus they would defcribe a battle, by painting two hands, one holding a fhield, the other a bow; a tumult, or popular infurrection, by an armed man cafting arrows; a fiege, by a fcaling ladder, &c. This from its fimplicity is fuppofed to be the earlieft, and is known by the name of the Curiologic Hieroglyphic. The fecond and more artificial contraction, was to fubftitute the inftrument of the thing, either real or metaphorical, for the thing itfelf. Thus an eye eminently placed, was intended to fignify God's omnifcience; an eye and fceptre, a monarch; a fhip and pilot, the Governor of the univerfe—and this is called the Tropical Hieroglyphic. The third refinement in this curious art, was to make one thing reprefent another, where any quaint refemblance or analogy in the reprefentative could be collected from their obfervations of nature, or their traditional fuperftition—and this was their Symbolic Hieroglyphic, and may be termed the art of painting by metaphor. To give fome inftances of this method of writing:—The univerfe was defigned by a ferpent in a circle, whofe variegated fpots fignified the ftars; in this cafe there is an analogy, though remote. A widow, who never admits a fecond mate, was reprefented by a black pigeon:—this is a juft and lively image of conftancy and grief. But when they defcribed the fun rifing, by the two eyes of a crocodile, the refemblance

appears

appears to me purely fanciful. A king, ftern and inexorable, is juftly figured by an eagle. A client, flying for relief to his patron, and finding none, is well expreffed by a fparrow and an owl. A wife, who hates her hufband; or children, who injure their mother, by a viper. A man, initiated into the myfteries, and under an obligation of fecrecy, by a grafshopper, becaufe that animal was thought to have no mouth. Such are the three forms of hiero-glyphics fo famous among the Egyptians. But without fuffering ourfelves to be involved in the intricacies of learning, let us endeavour to trace the progrefs of the human mind in its fucceffive im-provements in this moft wonderful art. The Curio-logic Hieroglyphic, is nothing more than an abridg-ment of the cuftom adopted by all nations, of painting the images of things, and can only exprefs thofe ideas which are derived from objects of fight— all thofe which depend on found, as well as abftract ideas of every fort, are excluded. The Tropical Hieroglyphic takes in a wider fphere, and expreffes fome abftract ideas by metaphorical images, as is the cuftom in the infancy of Language. The Sym-bolic goes yet further, and records by analogy, at-tributes, and moral modes. The great objection againft the Symbolic Hieroglyphic, is the ftudied obfcurity in which it is involved. This I conceive not to have been natural to it at its firft inftitution, but introduced by the priefts afterwards, to throw

F a veil

a veil of myftery over their religion and laws.
When men firft applied to this art of picture-writing,
they muft have found themfelves very much perplexed to defcribe the qualities of the perfon they
painted. The method they fixed on I conceive to be
this: they obferved in animals certain ftriking and
characteriftic qualities; fuch as fiercenefs in a tiger;
fidelity in a dog; conftancy in a dove; ingratitude
in a viper, &c. To apply thefe or any other qualities to particular perfons, they added to the human
figure already painted, the images of thofe animals
whofe qualities bore the greateft affinity to the characters they intended to defcribe. Afterwards, by contraction, the animal which was at firft defigned only to
exprefs the attribute, was made ufe of to exprefs both
the attribute and fubftance. This was the cafe in the
Symbolic Hieroglyphic, where in the inftance above
mentioned we fee a difconfolate widow reprefented by
a black pigeon; a ftern and inexorable prince, by an
eagle; and fometimes the moral modes, impudence,
uncleannefs, and deftruction, were expreffed by a fly,
a wild goat, and a moufe. Animals were introduced
at firft only to exprefs their more obvious and ftriking
qualities; but the Egyptians, who applied themfelves
very early to the ftudy of natural hiftory, befides
thefe, difcovered other fecondary and hidden qualities in animals, and, from the vanity of fcience,
made ufe of the fame image to exprefs the former as
the latter; and it is not uncommon to fee oppofite
qualities

qualities reprefented by the fame animal. This has involved the fcience of ancient hieroglyphic in almoft impenetrable obfcurity; and to render it yet more difficult, many of the qualities of their animals are imaginary. We have already feen fubftances and their attributes, and even abftract nouns, expreffed by hieroglyphics; but then they are disjointed and independent, and can never make parts of a continued difcourfe, without terms of connection and relation. To fupply this defect, they invented arbitrary marks, which were at firft ufed as connectives and relatives; afterwards they were employed to exprefs mental conceptions, and even qualities. The Chinefe went further, and rejecting the images, retained only the abitrary mark. This forms their famous character; and as every diftinct idea muft have its peculiar mark, the number is prodigious. The characters of Cochin, Tongking, and Japan, fays Du Halde, are the fame with thofe of China, and exprefs the fame ideas; although the languages are very different, and the people can fcarcely make themfelves underftood by one another in fpeaking, yet their books and letters are intelligible to all. This appears incredible to thofe who have never extended their views beyond alphabetic writing; but the reafon is obvious: the Chinefe characters are reprefentatives of things, alphabetic writing of words; the former in their nature are fixed and unchangeable, the latter fleeting and capricious. The cyphers in arithmetic,

which

which have the fame fignification, notwithſtanding the diverſity of language in every country in Europe, will convey no bad idea of the nature of the Chineſe charaĉters. The uſe of arbitrary marks to expreſs abſtraĉt ideas, has been no leſs generally adopted, than the uſe of images to expreſs things. The Mexicans, we are informed, were not unacquainted with them; and the Quippo's or knotted cords of the Peruvians, are of univerſal notoriety. Thus have we traced hieroglyphic writing from its moſt ſimple ſtate of expreſſing ideas by repreſentation, to the more refined one of analogy; till at length we ſee it abſorbed by marks of arbitrary inſtitution, which ſeem to hold a middle ſpace between hieroglyphic and alphabetic writing. The invention of the alphabet is ſo extremely artificial and ingenious, that Plato and Tully conceived it to be a diſcovery far beyond the powers of the human underſtanding, and ſuppoſed it to be a gift derived immediately from the gods. This certainly is an argument in favour of its antiquity. The Egyptians lay claim to this, as well as to almoſt every other uſeful diſcovery, and aſcribe the honour of it to Thoth. All that is related of this Thoth is involved in myſtery and fable; but ſuch is the vaſt diſtance between marks of arbitrary inſtitution repreſenting things, and charaĉters repreſenting ſounds, reſolvable into a literal alphabet as their elementary parts, that I conceive a diſcovery of this ſort to be too great for the limited under-

2   ſtanding

standing of man, unlefs affifted by fome prior invention; let us endeavour to mark out the progreffive fteps which led to this difcovery: I fuppofe
a man of fublime and comprehenfive genius, ftruck
with the obfcurity which was infeparable from the
hieroglyphic mode of writing by analogy, and the
endlefs labour of inventing a multitude of arbitrary
marks to reprefent things, from repeated obfervations
might be led to conclude, that by fubftituting marks
for founds inftead of things, the communication of
our thoughts might be rendered more clear and
eafy; that however difficult this undertaking might
appear, yet as the articulate founds uttered by man,
though infinitely varied, are by no means numerous,
it was far from impracticable to reduce them within
certain limits, and arrange them under certain
divifions. This gave rife to arbitrary marks, deno-
ting fimple founds, which I fhall call the Syllabic
Alphabet. This invention muft have been a wonderful effort of the human underftanding, and opened the way to a difcovery yet more extraordinary;
the art of refolving thofe fimple founds into vowels
and confonants, as their elementary parts. At firft
the literal alphabet muft, from its imperfect ftate,
have retained fome veftiges of the fyllabic; this I
conceive to have been the cafe of the greater part
of the Oriental Languages, before the ufe of vowel
points. We have no account of the name of the
inventor of this moft ufeful art, who fo well de-

ferved

ferved immortality, but what is contained in the
fabulous relations of the Egyptians, and hiſtory is
altogether ſilent as to the time of the invention.
Some writers ſuppoſe the alphabet to be a gift of
God beſtowed on the Iſraelites, and by them communicated to the Egyptians; but the firſt mention
we find of writing, is in Exodus, when Moſes received the decalogue written on two tables of ſtone,
by the finger of God. Had the Iſraelites at that
time been ignorant of alphabetic writing, they could
not have underſtood their laws without a revelation
from heaven, to explain the charaĉters in which they
were written. Yet the ſacred hiſtorian ſays nothing
of this revelation; and it is the height of abſurdity
to ſuppoſe that he would have been ſilent on a
ſubjeĉt of ſo great importance. We may therefore
conclude, that the Iſraelites were acquainted with
alphabetic writing before their departure from
Egypt; and the invention muſt have been prior to
their deſcent, or during their abode there. Scripture
will not juſtify the ſuppoſition, that the patriarchs knew
any thing of the alphabet, or indeed of any other
kind of writing; as we find communication carried
on by meſſengers, who delivered every thing by word
of mouth. I believe few people ſuppoſe that the
Egyptians had invented the alphabet before the arrival of the Iſraelites. It muſt therefore have
been diſcovered during the time of the abode of
that people in Egypt; and allowing it to be of human
invention,

invention, the honour is juftly due to the Egyptians; for it cannot be fuppofed that the Ifraelites, whilft labouring under the moft cruel oppreffions and in-fults, and occupied in continual labour, could fo far abftraɛt the mind, as to invent an art, which of all others, required the moft refined and metaphyfical reafoning.

Upon the whole we may conclude, that Mofes brought the alphabet from Egypt; but what im-provements it received from his hands afterwards, I pretend not to affirm. It appears extraordinary that the Egyptians, after the invention of the al-phabet, fhould yet retain the ufe of their hierogly-phics; but many reafons may be affigned for their conduɛt: Firft, their prejudice in favour of their an-cient cuftoms; the artifice of their priefts, who wifhed to throw a veil of myftery over the moft fublime truths of morality and religion, to attraɛt by that means the veneration of mankind; to conceal the fecrets of their religion and laws from the eyes of foreigners, and to prevent the wicked and prophane from par-ticipating in their religious rites. This will account for the ftudied obfcurity which univerfally prevails in the latter hieroglyphics, fo different from the fimplicity of the earlier; as it was the objeɛt of one to fecrete, the other to divulge. The Ifraelites were forbidden by the fecond commandment, to make ufe of hieroglyphics; the objeɛt of that
prohibition,

prohibition, was to preferve God's chofen people free from idolatry, to which the ufe of hieroglyphics had a fatal tendency; for when refined and obfcured by the myftic learning of their priefts, and employed as the only vehicle for the explanation of moral and religious truth, it infenfibly gave rife to thofe various forms of brute worfhip, to which the Egyptians were fo fuperftitioufly addicted. So ftrictly did the Ifraelites adhere to this law, that they marked their conftellations in the heavens, not by the fymbols of men and animals, as was the cuftom of every other nation, but by alphabetic characters.

Thus have I endeavoured to explain in as clear and concife a manner as I am able, the dark and perplexed fcience of hieroglyphics; if in any part I feem obfcure, or the reafons I urge appear unfatisfactory, I muft refer my reader to the late Dr. Warburton; who in the fourth book of his *divine legation of Mofes*, has treated this difficult fubject with that depth of learning and ftrength of judgment for which he was fo juftly celebrated.

The immediate confequence of the ufe of alphabetic writing, muft be the diffufion of knowledge. This the Egyptian priefts were fully convinced of, and therefore retained their hieroglyphics to keep the people in ignorance; but among nations, whofe fentiments were more liberal and generous, we find
this

this moft ufeful art applied to the noble purpofe of extending the influence of morality and religion. But in their firft compofitions, we muft expeft to fee them retain fomething of their ancient cuftom of hieroglyphic writing by analogy. This gave rife to fable, the moft ancient fpecies of writing, adopted by all nations, and allowed to be the beft vehicle, for conveying moral and political truths. The fimple fable was fucceeded by allegory, which is a more refined mode of communication. But when the imagination was warmed by the contemplation of the attributes of the Deity, his moral government of the univerfe, or by any fublime objeft in the natural world, and the underftanding laboured for expreffion, it is reafonable to believe they would copy in their writings, thofe hieroglyphic images by which they formerly communicated fimilar conceptions. This is remarkably exemplified in the prophetic writings in the Old Teftament; where we fee the fubverfion of cities and empires, fignified by the falling of the ftars, and the eclipfes of the fun and moon. It is well known that the cœleftial bodies were ufed by the Egyptians as hieroglyphic images, to reprefent kings, princes, and rulers. So many inftances of this fort occur in reading the prophets, that fome of our moft learned divines have emphatically ftyled them fpeaking Hieroglyphics. This, next to the intrinfic greatnefs of the fubjeft, may be affigned as a principal caufe of that boldnefs

G   and

and fublimity of imagery in which they muſt be acknowledged to excel all other writers.

From Egypt the Phœnicians received the alphabetic character, and had the honour of communicating that moſt uſeful diſcovery to the Greeks. Cadmus is ſaid to have brought with him ſixteen of the twenty-four letters which formed their alphabet; nor was this gift loſt upon the Greeks: the ſame ſuperiority of genius appeared in their language as in their works of art. If we examine its ſtrength, copiouſneſs, regularity, and harmony, we ſhall find it equally excellent in every part. This will beſt appear by taking a ſhort view of their writers, and we will begin with the poets, who are the firſt in order of time.

We find in Homer all that can ſtrike the imagination, awaken the paſſions, or inform the judgment: like a ſuperior being he ſurveys all nature in one comprehenſive view—penetrates into the deepeſt receſſes of the human heart, and marks the infinite variety under which it appears. Not leſs bold in his expreſſions, than ſublime in his ſentiments, when he deſcribes the majeſty of a god, or the horrors of a battle: but, when he paints the calm and ſequeſtered ſcenes, and the amiable virtues of private life, ſimplicity and eaſe, elegance and ſweetneſs, appear in every line. In the choice and diſ-
poſition

pofition of his words; in the juftnefs of his meta-
phors; and in the arrangement of the various parts
of his work.—I fay in thefe, as well as in every
other excellence, he yet remains and probably will
ever remain unequalled. The ftyle of Hefiod is
fuited to his fubject, which is rural and didactic; he
never rifes to the fublime, or amufes his reader with
the luxuriance of poetic defcription; but he merits
a large portion of praife, for the juftnefs of his precepts, the fimplicity of his diction, the harmony
of his periods, and the regularity of his compofition.

In the lyric poems of Alcæus, we fee a boldnefs
and vigour of thought, and a ftrength and brevity
of expreffion.

In Sappho, who well deferved the name of the
tenth mufe, we behold a delicacy of fentiment, and
an elegance of ftyle well fitted to defcribe the
tender paffions, and the finer feelings of the human
foul.

In Pindar, every thing is great and magnificent;
we are ftruck with the elevation of his thoughts, the
fplendour of his words, the boldnefs of his figures,
and that copious and rapid ftream of eloquence
which carries all before it.

Æfchylus,

Æfchylus, the renowned father of tragic poetry, is warm, energetic, and fublime; never fo great as when he defcribes fcenes of horror, and paints the fad effects of wild and ungoverned paffions.

We admire the calm dignity of Sophocles, well fkilled to touch the human foul, and call forth all the virtuous and tender affections.

The tear ftarts from the eye whilft we perufe the pathetic ftrains of Euripedes.—In all things admirable; but, particularly excellent in exciting the paffion of pity.

If we turn our eyes from their poets to their hiftorians; we fhall fee in Herodotus, grace, elegance, and harmony; a flowing and copious eloquence, an artful arrangement of periods, and a lucid order in the difpofition of his facts.

Thucydides, is folemn, grave, and pathetic; firmly attached to the facred caufe of truth and virtue, he is lefs attentive to the cadence of his periods than to the dignity of his fubject, which he ennobles by the native elevation of his mind. In his fentiments fublime, in his diction figurative and poetical.—Here the ftatefman may find the beft maxims of political wifdom; the orator the nobleft examples of warm and perfuafive eloquence, and

the

the patriot the moſt animating motives to excite him to prefer the public good to every private and ſelfiſh conſideration.

Simplicity, perſpicuity, and unaffected ſweetneſs, characterize the ſtyle of Xenophon. The ancients ſaid, that the goddeſs of perſuaſion had ſeated herſelf on his lips: ſparing in the uſe of figures and other rhetorical ornaments, he builds his reputation on the juſtneſs of his ſentiments, and his warm and ardent love for religion and virtue. Formed by the inſtructions of the immortal Socrates, and endowed by nature with the happieſt diſpoſitions, as a ſoldier, hiſtorian, and philoſopher, he was equally admirable; and may boaſt the honour of delivering the doctrines of his great maſter, more pure than any of his other diſciples.

Who will diſpute the palm of oratory with Greece, whilſt they boaſt a Demoſthenes? In him we behold ſuch wonderful powers of argument; ſuch ſtrong and nervous expreſſions; and on proper occaſions ſuch bold and animated addreſſes to the paſſions, that the reader reſts ſatisfied; convinced that in him there is nothing either deficient or redundant. This great man employed his ſuperior talents in a glorious attempt to relume the expiring virtue of his country, and for ſome time ſuſpended her fall.

Æſchinus,

Æschinus, who holds the fecond rank, is more figurative and diffufe; inferior to Demofthenes in the vigour and ftrength of his genius, inftead of informing the underftanding, or moving the paffions, he too frequently plays with the imagination.

Plato, the prince of moral philofophers, holds a diftinguifhed place among orators; and I believe I fhould not go too far, to affirm, that the funeral oration of Menexenus, is the nobleft profe compofition that ever flowed from an uninfpired pen.

It may not be amifs to obferve in this place, that fuch is the excellence of the Greek Language, that it is equally adapted to every fubject treated of by the authors I have juft now mentioned; and we may venture to affert, that in poetry, hiftory, and eloquence of every kind, the Greeks in the age of Alexander the Great, were infinitely our fuperiors.

HEATHEN

HEATHEN MYTHOLOGY

AND

MORAL PHILOSOPHY.

I HAVE obferved in a former diſſertation, that
the fun and moon from their fplendour and apparent utility, were the firſt objeſts of adoration
among mankind ; for the fame caufe, the ſtars were
afterwards regarded as gods ; and the elements, the
air, fire, water, and earth, were not only worſhipped
by the Egyptians, Grecians, and the more enlightened nations of antiquity, by various names ex-
preſſive of their various qualities, but are now
adored by the uncivilized tribes of North-America.
The ordinary operations of nature, in violent guſts
of wind, in heavy rains, and above all in thunder-
ſtorms, muſt fill the mind of a favage with terror.
Unable to account philoſophically for theſe appearances, he is led by fuperſtition, the offspring of
ignorance and fear, to fuppofe a deity reſiding in
every ſtorm : this gives rife to the belief of an inferior kind of gods or genii ; by whom the various
phænomena in the elements are produced. Under
theſe

thefe three heads, viz. Star, Elementary, and Me-
terological Worfhip, may be included the religion
of mankind in their moft uncultivated ftate; whilft
fubfifting on the fpontaneous fruits of the earth, or
hunting, or fifhing. I am not ignorant, that it is
the opinion of many refpe&table writers, that the
appearance of nature, in which the power, wifdom,
and goodnefs of God are exprcffed in fuch ftrong
chara&ers, muft lead man in his moft favage ftate to
the knowledge of one God, the Creator and Father
of all things; but this is to fuppofe in a favage not
only the capacity for, but the habit of refle&ion;
than which nothing can be more contrary to his
chara&er. Mortifying as it is to our pride, it muft be
confeffed that many nations have been difcovered,
who have fcarcely had the leaft trace of an abftra&
idea. Is it not, therefore, more natural, that a
favage fhould fuppofe the univerfe to be governed
by obje&s of fenfe, whofe power and influence he
daily felt; than to feek for a remote caufe difcoverable only by long and abftra& reafoning.—That the
firft man had the knowledge of one God is undeniable, but that knowledge was the confequence
of a revelation: that the belief of the unity of
the Deity, was always preferved in one family,
which afterwards became a great nation, is a truth,
confirmed by the concurrent teftimony of facred
and prophane hiftorians: but the hiftory of this
people is one continued miracle, and their frequent
lapfes

lapfes into idolatry are a melancholy teftimony of the pronenefs of human nature to Polytheifm. Whenever I fpeak of man in his firft ftate, or as it is called by fome modern philofophers, the ftate of nature, I muft defire the reader not to fuppofe that I refer to the creation, when man came out of his Maker's hand, *perfect*; but to that period of barbarifm and darknefs, which overfpread the greateft part of the world after the difperfion of mankind at the tower of Babel. The monuments of the art and induftry of the antediluvian world, perifhed in the general flood; and the traces of knowledge in agriculture and the moft neceffary arts which had been preferved by Noah, and his defcendants, were foon after the above-mentioned difperfion, loft among the greater part of mankind: this, extraordinary as it may appear, is eafily accounted for; as they were ignorant of every kind of writing, they had no means of recording their ideas, or of extending their knowledge beyond the term of their natural life. The feeble light of tradition muft have been foon extinguifhed by their long migrations, in which vaft numbers muft have perifhed by their frequent wars, before they obtained a fettlement; and above all, by the difficulty of procuring fubfiftence, which muft have been fo great as to occupy every thought, and fix the attention of man folely on his immediate prefervation.

II   In

In the next stage of society, as the life of a shep-
herd affords more leisure than that of a hunter, so
it is more favourable for the exertion of the mental
powers.   Conversant day and night with the most
sublime objects in nature, a man may be led from
an observation of the regularity of the motions of
the heavenly bodies, the consequent uniform course
of the seasons, and that harmonious concert by
which every part of the creation is held together,
as it were in a golden chain, to suppose that all
this could not be effected but by the unerring hand
of Infinite Wisdom : from whence he forms an idea
of one God, Father and Lord of the universe.
Thus we find Job, who was doubtless an Arabian
and who led a pastoral life, profess his belief of the
unity of the Deity in opposition to star and elementary worship ; but by that opposition it appears, that the generality of his countrymen were
sunk in Polytheism.   It is said by Dr. Hyde, that
the Persians, from the earliest times, worshipped
one god under the symbol of Fire ; favoured by
nature with a mild climate and a fertile soil, their
country seems to have been peculiarly adapted to a
pastoral life ; and as I have observed before, contemplative minds in such a country, and in such a
state of society, might arrive at the knowledge of
the true God : but this knowledge could only prevail among men of improved understandings.   The
bulk of the nation, I conceive, were plunged as
                                              deep

deep in ftar and elementary worfhip as their
neighbours. Certain it is, no people ever adored the
fun with greater devotion, or were more fuperftitioufly addicted to divination from the ftars. Genii
and dæmons likewife made a favourite part of their
religion. It muft be confeffed that they regarded
with abhorrence every fpecies of image worfhip,
which has led many perfons to think more favour-
ably of their religion than it deferves. But during
the two firft ftages of fociety already defcribed, the
objects of worfhip are not eafily reprefented by any
artificial images ; and the imitative arts had, as yet,
made but very little progrefs among mankind. Tacitus, in his admirable treatife on the manners of the
ancient Germans, informs us, that they held it impious to endeavour to confine their gods within
walls, or to reprefent them by images framed in the
likenefs of the human form ; and we are likewife
told by Varro, that for the firft hundred and
feventy years after Romulus, there was no ftatue to
be found in Rome.

Image worfhip took its rife from the cuftom adopted by moft nations of adoring dead men ; but, as
thefe men were at firft legiflators, who by good and
wife laws had led mankind to defert the foreft and
the plain, to tafte the fweets of well-ordered fociety ;
or thofe other benefactors of their fellow-creatures,
who by the invention of new arts had contributed to

render life more comfortable and happy, image worſhip could never take place till after ſocieties were regularly formed, governments eſtabliſhed, and the arts cultivated, at leaſt, to a certain degree. We muſt therefore trace its origin from Egypt, that celebrated nurſe of the arts, and parent of ſuperſti-tion. Many circumſtances contributed to unite the Egyptians under a regular form of government at a very early period: their country deſtitute of wood, as it affords no ſhelter for beaſts of chace, could not long be a fit habitation for the hunter; the ſhepherd indeed might be tempted by the fer-tility of the ſoil, to feed his flocks in their rich paſtures, but then the periodical overflowings of the Nile would deſtroy all his hopes, and that part of his flock which eſcaped the general deſtruction, he muſt neceſſarily lead into the higher lands, and patiently wait till the waters abated.

To erect buildings for houſing the cattle, to provide ſubſiſtence for them during the annual inundation, to cut canals to break the force of the torrents, to raiſe higher banks to prevent its overflowing their towns and villages; all theſe things could not be done, but by the united labours of mankind under the direction of an eſtabliſhed government; yet without theſe precautions Egypt could not be ren-dered even habitable. But in this country, as ne-ceſſity awakened the induſtry of man, ſo the wonder-

ful

ful fertility of the foil, impregnated by the rich
waters of the Nile, made him ample amends for his
labour. We muſt not therefore be furprifed, that,
impelled by fuch powerful motives, the Egyptians
ſhould be the firſt people not only to form themfelves
into a regular fociety, but to adorn that fociety by
laws, religion, and arts. They made it their boaſt
(as we learn from Herodotus) that they were the
firſt people who built temples, raifed altars, and
erected ſtatues to their gods: that the fun and moon
were the firſt objects of their worſhip appears from
Diodorus Siculus, who fays, that they worſhipped
the former under the name of Ofiris, which fignifies many-eyed, by which they meant to exprefs the
all-pervading power of that glorious luminary ; the
latter they termed Ifis, and reprefented her with
horns, in allufion to the crefcent figure ſhe aſſumes
whilſt her ſtation is in the quadratures. Thefe two
deities they faid governed the world and prefided
over the feafons, on whofe regular and unalterable
return depended the beauty and harmony of the
univerfe ; they went yet further, and afcribed to
their divine influence the generation, not only of
plants but animals. The elements were not deified;
and the Egyptians fuppofed that the gods frequently
appeared among men, veiling their divinity under a
human and fometimes even a brute form : this
opinion, which firſt took its rife in Egypt and was
afterwards communicated to Greece, may be confidered

dered as the fource of thofe beautiful fables which corrupted the fimplicity of religion, by dreffing her in the robes of fancy; from hence too is derived the Mythology of the ancients, a term, which, in its moft extenfive fenfe, fignifies teaching by fable; but in its more limited and particular meaning, is confined to thofe fabulous relations under which the Egyptians and Greeks veiled their moft folemn rites of religion, and the moft important truths in Natural and Moral Philofophy: befides the deities already mentioned, which by way of dif-tinction are termed celeftial, the Egyptians had other gods of an inferior nature, which they called terreftrial; thefe were of mortal birth, benefactors to mankind, who, as legiflators, heroes, and inven-tors of ufeful arts, were beloved and reverenced whilft living, for their fuperior talents and tranfcen-dant virtue, and as they were fuppofed to have been animated by more than an ordinary portion of divi-nity; after their deceafe they were ranked in the number of their gods.—Fear, according to fome celebrated writers, is the parent of devotion; but in the worfhip of deified heroes, however it may be miftaken in its object, it certainly flows from a nobler principle—that of gratitude. The Egyptians gave to their firft heroes and legiflators, the names of their celeftial gods; and we find Ofiris and Ifis, celebrated as inventors of laws, agriculture, and the ufeful arts: Hermes, or Mercury, another

of

of their great men, is said to have reduced their
language to rules, to have enlarged it by the introduction of new words, and above all to have invented hieroglyphic writing. The Egyptians, who
from the earliest times were fond of conveying their
knowledge in mysterious language, personified not
only matter, spirit, and their various attributes, but
even mental qualities. This considerably enlarged
the number of their deities, and when involved in
the obscurity of allegory and adorned by the fiction
of poetry, presents to our view a system confused
and irregular; for it is not easy to discover in some
places, where the allegory ends and the history
begins: not to mention that men of the greatest
learning, and even soberest understanding, have
been led astray by a fancied similitude of terms, and
wandered through the mazes of error, without any
guide, but uncertain etymology, to direct them.

Besides the divinities already mentioned, which
have prevailed in part among all the nations of the
world, God's chosen people excepted, the Egyptians
had others that were peculiar to themselves. Such
were the sacred animals and plants, to which temples were erected and divine honours paid. To a
reflecting mind it must afford matter of astonish-
ment, to behold the most enlightened nation of
antiquity, so celebrated for the wisdom of its laws
and regularity of its government, fall down and

adore

adore the inferior parts of the creation. The learned have taken no fmall pains to account for this
apparent inconfiftency of conduct: fome fuppofe
that the beafts of the greateft utility to mankind
were felected for worfhip, and inftance the ox Apis,
which was regarded with particular reverence for
the fervice that animal was of in agriculture: but
thefe gentlemen ought to confider, that not only
ufeful, but noxious animals were adored; of this
we have an example in the crocodile. Befides, as
the utility of tame animals is not partial, but univerfal; why fhould brute worfhip be confined to
Egypt, and never prevail in any other part of the
world? fince the fame caufe muft every where produce the fame effect. Others attribute it to their
doctrine of the tranfmigration of fouls; but it may
well be difputed, whether brute worfhip was not
prior to that doctrine: I am rather inclined to
think it was; fince the Ifraelites, whofe attachment
to the Egyptian fuperftitions was fo ftrong, that the
miraculous difplay of the power and majefty of the
Deity, accompanied with a long ceremonial law,
could not prevent their frequent relapfes into
idolatry: yet we find no account of their once en-
tertaining an idea of the tranfmigration of fouls,
neither is there any pofitive law againft it; thofe in
my opinion are more judicious, who afcribe brute
worfhip to hieroglyphic writing. The Egyptians
reprefented not only human qualities, but divine

attributes

attributes, by figures of animals and plants: the analogy was always remote, and difguifed by fome fabulous relation, or allegoric myftery. The vulgar, immerfed in objects of fenfe, from their inability to penetrate the thick clouds, in which oftentatious fcience had involved the throne of truth, miftook the fymbol for the Deity, and firft adored the picture or image of the animal, afterwards the animal itfelf. This will account for the rife of brute worfhip among the Egyptians; this will likewife account for its never extending beyond the limits of that country: for although hieroglyphic writing by reprefentation, and even by analogy, has prevailed in every part of the world, yet no where was it carried to that degree of refinement, no where involved in fuch ftudied obfcurity, or difguifed by fuch remote and diftant allufions, as among the Egyptians.

The Greeks derived their religion from Egypt. If we confult the Orphic Hymns, or Hefiod's Theogony, we fhall find long genealogies of elementary gods, and defcriptions of their operations in the formation of the world out of chaos; adorned by the lively colouring of Grecian fancy. Dr. Burnet, in his ingenious though fanciful theory of the earth, obferves, that the Grecian account of the creation, though it bears the appearance of a poetic fiction, is founded on found philofophy, and

I   very

very nearly refembles the account given by Mofes. This is not furprifing, when we confider that the opinions of mankind on thofe operations of nature which are the objects of fenfe, muft be nearly the fame; to which I may add, that Mofes, as well as the Greeks, was indebted to Egypt for his learning, and the philofophy of both was probably derived from the fame fource. The fymbol of the mundane egg (afcribed to Orpheus); in a word, the whole of the firft religion which prevailed in Greece, was purely elementary, and muft be confidered as of Egyptian original.

Tully obferves, that the ancient theologifts reckon three Jupiters; of whom, the firft and fecond were born in Arcadia, and had for their fathers, Æther, and Cælus; the third was a native of Crete, and the fon of Saturn. If we confider, that by Cælus is underftood, the Heaven, by Æther, the Air, and by Saturn, Time; it is not difficult to explain the genealogy of this elementary deity: by the incubation of the heaven, or celeftial fire on Æther, and by the agency of Saturn or Time, is produced that vivid principle which the ancients fuppofed to be diffufed through all nature; and by whofe divine influence all things animate or inanimate were generated. As allegory and fable can affume a thoufand forms, fo we have various accounts of the birth of Jupiter: the moft received, is, that he was the
                                        youngeft

youngeft fon of Saturn, or Time, by Rhea; that his cruel parent had fwallowed up all his former progeny; that is, that time had covered them with the veil of oblivion; that Jupiter, when he was grown to man's eftate, warred with the Titans, or jarring elements of Chaos, after many conflicts fubdued them, fixed himfelf on the throne of his anceftors, eftablifhed peace and harmony, and dif-pofed and governed every thing in the world by the fixed and unalterable dictates of Divine Wifdom: this allegory is too plain to require an explanation. In the fame manner they reprefent Juno, or the Air, as the fifter and the wife of Jupiter; born of the fame parents, Saturn and Rhea: as by Jupiter is underftood the active or creative, fo by Juno is underftood the recipient, or productive principle. A perfon muft be no lefs ignorant of philofophy, than dead to the charms of poetry, who is not ftruck with the beauty of this fable.

By preferving this idea of Jupiter and Juno, we fhall not be offended at their frequent contefts, but reft fatisfied, that from the convulfion of jarring elements the vigour of nature is reftored, and the order and harmony of the univerfe preferved; Juno will then appear in her proper department, as the patronefs of marriage: even the various tranf-formations of her fpoufe, will ceafe to fhock us when we regard him as the principle of life and

generation,

generation, and reflect on the various means the God of nature makes ufe of, to accomplifh his ends.

/ The claffical reader may perufe the metamor-phofes of Ovid with no lefs profit than pleafure; when he confiders that, that wonderful book is not only adorned with all the luxuriance of poetic de-fcription, but contains, under the veil of fable, the principles of natural philofophy and religion which prevailed in the ancient world. Before I leave the regions of allegory, I muft trefpafs fo far on the reader's patience, as to take fome notice of the ftory of Prometheus.—We are informed that this extraordinary perfonage finding mankind rude, bar-barous, and perifhing for want of the neceffaries of life; in compaffion to their diftrefs, contrived to afcend to heaven; and lighting his torch at the chariot-wheel of the fun, conveyed the celeftial fire to earth, and made a prefent of it to man. A change of affairs immediately took place: metals were difcovered and worked, in confequence of the invention of fire; tools were formed; houfes were built; and land cultivated: the return of the feafons afcertained by aftronomical obfervations; ideas communicated by vifible marks; in fhort, every invention by which the neceffities of man might be fupplied, or his nature adorned, is afcribed to the tranfcendent wifdom and benevolence of Prome-

theus.

theus. We are afterwards told that Jupiter incenfed
againſt him for the compaſſion he had ſhewn to
man, fixed him by chains to mount Caucaſus, where
Vultures for ever preyed on his liver. This appears,
at firſt fight, to be a cruel return for ſuch unexam-
pled goodneſs; but let us examine the fable more
cloſely : by Prometheus is meant Foreſight; he was
the fon of Japetus and Themis (Deſire and Deſtiny);
he brought down fire from heaven; i. e. he diſcovered fire, and applied it to uſeful purpoſes; he
civilized mankind, ſupplied their wants, and invented every art and ſcience : all this is the effect
of foreſight.—He is tormented by Vultures which
perpetually gnaw his liver: what are thoſe vultures
but thoſe corroding thoughts which for ever diſtract
the anxious and reflecting mind ? Can any allegory
be more juſt and beautiful ? It is foreſight which
principally diſtinguiſhes the member of civil ſociety
from the uncultivated ſavage. As the latter too
often degenerates into a careleſs inattention to fu-
turity, even to a neglect of providing common ne-
ceſſaries ; ſo the former too frequently a ſlave to
ambition and avarice, vainly endeavours to give a
perpetuity to what is in its nature fleeting and incon-
ſtant, and renders his life miſerable by indulging
anxious and unneceſſary cares.

The Greeks, after the example of their maſters the
Egyptians, ſoon learnt to deify their heroes. Many
of the exploits attributed to Jupiter, like thoſe aſcribed

cribed to Ofiris, fuch as the civilization of mankind, the eftablifhment of laws, and the invention of arts, feem better fuited to the chara&er of an enlightened mortal, than an elementary deity; and probably that name was beftowed, by way of diftin&ion, on the firft legiflators in Greece. This will reconcile the various and difcordant accounts of their Mythologifts; who reprefent Jupiter as a native of Bæotia, Arcadia, and Crete.

Bacchus, his reputed fon, was held in the higheft veneration for the important difcoveries he communicated to mankind: he firft inftru&ed them in the culture of the vine, eftablifhed good laws, and extended his voyages through the greateft part of the known world; a&uated by the laudable ambition of imparting the fweets of fociety to the moft diftant nations.

Ceres, who, according to Sir Ifaac Newton, was a native of Sicily, arriving in Attica, taught the Greeks to fow corn; for which benefa&ion fhe was deified after her death. The nine minftrels who accompanied the Egyptian Ofiris in his expedition, were confidered by the Greeks as the inventors of mufic and poetry, and honoured by them as deities under the name of the nine mufes. As in the early ftages of fociety, mufic and poetry were the only vehicles of knowledge, they were faid to prefide
over

over every art and fcience, and have names affigned them expreffive of their different charaɛters. Hercules, for his ftrength and courage, which were always generoufly exerted for the good of his fellow-creatures, received divine honours after his death. Æfculapius, the inventor of medicine, was no lefs reverenced. To give a particular account of all the heroes the fuperftitious admiration of the Greeks deified, would far exceed the limits of this differtation; let it then fuffice to obferve, that fuch was the paffion of that people for hero worfhip, that they paid divine honours to every man after his deceafe, who was endowed with fuperior talents, or who gave extraordinary difplays of wifdom, valour, and juftice. But a due attention to the Mythology of Greece, will tend to reconcile the two opinions which have fo long divided the learned world refpeɛting the nature of their deities: fome holding them to be purely elementary, others regarding them all, without diftiɛtion, as deified heroes.

In the firft ftages of fociety, the deities of Greece, liké thofe of every other nation under the fame circumftances, were purely elementary; and as fuch are defcribed by Orpheus and Hefiod, their earlieft Mythologifts. But afterwards, when fociety was improved by the introduɛtion of laws, and the invention of arts, thofe perfons who had been enabled to form a juft idea of the advantages of civil fociety,

by

by comparing it with the barbarous state from which they had just emerged, thought they could never sufficiently honour those extraordinary men, to whom they were indebted for such signal blessings: legislators, who by their wisdom formed; heroes, who by their courage supported; and the inventors of useful arts, who by their ingenuity adorned society, were enrolled among their gods. The same principle of gratitude which first taught them to adore the sun as the fountain of light, and the source of life, made them regard with no less reverence the inventors of laws and the dispensers of justice; and in the latter worship the former was at length absorbed. For man in the refinement of society, as he is less conversant with nature, so is he less attentive to her operations; consequently he will be less addicted to elementary worship: to which I may add, that philosophy, by assigning causes for those appearances of nature, which to an uninformed mind are most terrible and potentous, must dissolve the charm which had so long amused the fancy. Besides the worship paid in general to their deified heroes, the Egyptians and Greeks established mysteries, which were every year celebrated with great solemnity: the most remarkable in Greece, were the Eleusinian, instituted by Eumolpus in honour of Ceres, not long after her decease. In these mysteries, the initiated were instructed in those truths, which, from their nature and

importance,

importance, were moſt likely to form the mind to
the practice of virtue. The immortality of the ſoul,
and the ſtate of future rewards and puniſhments,
were not only ſtrongly inculcated by words, but figured
by a ſhadowy repreſentation of the poets Tartarus
and Elizium. Perſons of immoral characters were
excluded from a participation in thoſe ſacred rites.
Nothing on the part of the prieſts was omitted to fill
the mind of the initiated with religious awe, and prepare it for the reception of thoſe important ſecrets
which were gradually unfolded to them. To ſtrike
the greater horror, they were conducted into a dark
room, ſtrange and myſterious voices were heard; at
length light began to dawn, which juſt enabled them
to diſcern the ſcenical repreſentation above alluded
to. To prevent a profanation of theſe myſteries,
all the initiated bound themſelves by a ſolemn oath,
never to reveal what they had ſeen or heard. By
every thing that is known at this diſtance of time
on a ſubject in its own nature ſo obſcure, it appears,
that of all the expedients which the moſt enlightened
of the Heathen world have ever fixed upon for
teaching their fellow-creatures the duty they owed
to God, to their country, and to themſelves, this,
as it was the moſt extraordinary, proved the moſt
effectual. Here the initiated beheld torments in-
flicted on tyrants who enſlaved, or traitors who be-
trayed their country; on men who by their power
ſet at defiance, or by their artifice evaded the ſword

K

of

of juſtice.   Here perfidy and ingratitude, envy and
avarice, though not cognizable by human laws, met
with their juſt reward.   Such were the Eleuſinian
myſteries, at their firſt inſtitution ; but as their cele-
bration was accompanied with games, muſic, feaſt-
ing, and dancing, the vulgar, as it frequently hap-
pens in their expreſſions of joy, exceeded the bounds
of temperance.   This gave riſe to many diſorders,
which infected and diſhonoured their religion.   To
remedy this inconvenience, they eſtabliſhed other
myſteries, which were termed the greater.—None
were admitted to theſe laſt but thoſe who by their
wiſdom, birth, and virtue, were judged worthy of
being intruſted with a ſecret of the greateſt importance, which indeed ſtruck at the root of their religion and government.   This ſecret is ſaid to be
nothing leſs than the unity of the Deity.—The initiated after paſſing through the former myſteries,
were informed, that all which they had before ſeen,
related to perſons who had been long ſince dead,
and were only deified in compliance with the prejudices of the vulgar.—That true religion conſiſted
in the knowledge and worſhip of one God, Creator
and Father of all things.   A late writer, whoſe
learning was equalled only by his genius, in his
Criticiſm on the ſixth book of Virgil, has favoured
the world with a full account of theſe myſteries,
of which I have here given only an imperfect ſketch.

For

For a long time the myfteries were preferved in their original purity; and when (according to the nature of all things *human*) they became depraved and corrupted, even in their worft ftate, they were not without a beneficial influence on the morals of the people; many by initiation were then reclaimed from a vicious courfe of life.

But it muft be confeffed for the honour of Paganifm, that the more enlightened Heathens amid their multiplicity of deities, acknowledged one fupreme God alone, felf-exiftent, the Creator and Father of all things; and this was not only the opinion of Socrates, Plato, and thofe philofophers who flourifhed when the Arts and Sciences were highly cultivated, and the refinements of life carried to the higheft degree of poffible perfeftion, but appears to have been ftrongly inculcated by Orpheus, Hefiod, and Homer, their earlieft Mythologifts.—Zeus or Jupiter is ftyled by Orpheus, The Original and King of all things.—" There is one Power, and one " God, and one great Ruler over all," fays that great poet. Hefiod likewife terms Jupiter, " The " Father and the King of the gods." And Homer calls him, " The moft powerful of all, the firft and " chiefeft of the gods, and the Father of gods and " men." The attribute of Omnipotence contained in thefe expreffions, is in its nature incommunicable; and confequently applicable only to one Supreme Being

K 2   eternal

eternal and felf-exiftent: confequently, the inferior
deities adored by the Pagans, were not regarded by
them as independent principles of nature, but as
created beings, in power and excellence fuperior to
man, who derived their birth from one common
fource, and were the children of one common
Father.   Thefe fubordinate cœleftial gods, as I have.
obferved before, were the works of nature, the
moral qualities, and the divine attributes, perfonified;
and may be confidered as the minifters of the will,
or the manifeftation of the goodnefs, wifdom, and
power of one Supreme God. .This Polytheifm,
which together with the unity of the Deity, was
derived from Egypt, proceeded at firft from an inadequate conception of his attributes.   This is well
explained by the beautiful allegory of Ofiris cut in
pieces by Typhon : " Ifis, fays Plutarch, is a Greek
" word which fignifies knowledge, and Typhon is
" the enemy to this goddefs, who being puffed up
" by ignorance and error, doth diftract the holy
" doctrine of the fimple deity, which Ifis collects
" together again and makes up into one, and thus
" delivers it to thofe who are initiated into her facred
" myfteries in order to deification."   By this it appears, that the meaning of the Egyptian fable is, that
the idea of the unity of the Deity was obfcured by
the weaknefs of mankind, who, unable to comprehend Infinite Perfection, difhonoured him by their
partial and imperfect notions of his nature, which
                                                    yet

yet true wifdom, that is, Ifis, unites together and, from many inadequate conceptions, forms a juft and true idea of his being and attributes. What confiderably increafed the number of the Pagan deities, was the old philofophic principle, that God is in all things, or that the Divine Nature pervades the whole creation. This, like moft of the Grecian doctrines, was derived from Egypt, where Neith, or Athena, is thus defcribed, I am all that was, is, and fhall be, and my veil no mortal fhall uncover. This doctrine (which fignifies nothing more than the omniprefence or fuperintendance of the Deity) imperfectly underftood, led them to fill every grove, mountain, and river, with an innumerable fwarm of local or tutelar deities. This humour was much encouraged by their poets, who by animating every, even the minuteft parts of nature, gave a warmth and vigour to their poems, which the moderns muft never expect to equal.

Varro, the moft learned of all the Romans, diftinguifhes three kinds of theology; the firft, mythical, or fabulous; the fecond, philofophical, or natural; the third, civil, or popular. In the former part of this differtation, I have principally enlarged on the firft and third, and it may not be improper in this place to fay fomething of the fecond, or philofohical, which Varro conceived to be far above the capacity of vulgar citizens;

citizens; for he affirms, that there are many truths in religion which ought to be concealed from the vulgar; and that there are some things which, though false, it was expedient for them to believe.

If we examine the opinions of Pythagoras, Socrates, Plato, Ariſtotle, and the moſt celebrated philoſophers of antiquity, on this moſt important ſubjeɛt, we ſhall find, that they acknowledged one God, all-perfeɛt, and ſelf-exiſtent, together with many other inferior and created gods; that however they might differ as to the number or quality of theſe ſubordinate deities, they agreed in ſuppoſing them to be intelleɛtual beings ſuperior to men, preſiding over different parts of the univerſe; who, as miniſters of the Supreme God, were entitled to honour and worſhip: and whether they conſidered them as animated ſubſtances, or as abſtraɛt qualities, they adored them as emanations of that divine mind, which is alone eternal and uncreated.

But what may ſeem extraordinary to thoſe who have been accuſtomed to look down with contempt on the wiſdom of the Pagan world; we find that the enlightened ancients, beſides the unity of the Deity, believed a trinity of divine hypoſtaſes. Orpheus, Pythagoras, and Plato, were the great ſupporters of this opinion in Greece: as they were indebted to Egypt for the beſt part of their philoſophy,

fophy, it is probable that this myfterious doctrine was derived from that great ftorehoufe of ancient learning. Many of our graveft and moft learned divines, fuppofe it to have been communicated to the Egyptians by the Ifraelites ;—an opinion I prefume not to conteft. Certain it is that this doctrine is very ancient, and it is not eafy to conceive by what means human reafon could arrive at the knowledge of fo great a myftery, without a divine revelation. The learned Dr. Cudworth has made it appear, that the three Platonic hypóftafes τἀγαθον, νοͻς, και ψυχη, which fignify infinite goodnefs, infinite wifdom, and infinite active power and love; not as mere qualities or accidents, but as fubftantial things, all concurring to make up one Θειον or Divinity; approaches very nearly to the Chriftian doctrine of the Trinity, firft, to ufe the words of this great man, in not making a mere trinity of names and words, or of logical notions, or inadequate conceptions of one and the fame thing; but a trinity of hypoftafes, or fubftances, or perfons; fecondly, in making none of their three hypoftafes to be creatures, but all eternal, neceffarily exiftent, and univerfal, omnipotent, and creators of the whole world ; laftly, in fuppofing thefe three divine hypoftafes, however fometimes Paganically called three gods, to be effentially one divinity. Thus far the Chriftian and Platonic Trinities agree, and I muft beg leave to decline the tafk of pointing out the particulars in
which

which they differ; as it would neceſſarily lead me into a long train of abſtruſe and metaphyſical reaſoning, which would be attended with little pleaſure or profit to the reader. Let us rather expreſs our admiration of the divine providence of God, that this myſterious doctrine of the Trinity ſhould find ſuch eaſy admittance in the Pagan world, and prepare the way for the reception of Chriſtianity. It may likewiſe check the pride of thoſe ſuperficial reaſoners, who, becauſe they cannot comprehend the aſtoniſhing depth and height of the knowledge and wiſdom of God, preſume to cenſure the doctrine of the Trinity as contradictory to our reaſon, when they find it received by the wiſeſt and beſt philoſophers among the Pagans before the time of Chriſtianity. I muſt requeſt the reader to take notice, that what I have ſaid of the Platonic Trinity is applicable only to it as it was delivered by Plato in its original purity; that it was much altered by his diſciples I readily admit, and the latter Platoniſts ſo far degenerated from their maſter, as to make this ſublime doctrine, which ſeems ſo well calculated to convey clear and juſt conceptions of the Deity, the ſource of ſtrange fables, and impious inquiries; where the perception of truth was obſcured by the ambiguity of language, and human reaſon itſelf loſt in the mazes of ſophiſtical argumentation. I ſhould think myſelf unjuſt if I did not in this place acknowledge my obligations to Dr. Cudworth's

3   Intellectual

Intellectual Syſtem, from which excellent book I have extracted many paſſages in this diſſertation.

If we obſerve the conduct of thoſe legiſlators who are moſt renowned in hiſtory, we ſhall find them uniform in their attempts to enforce their laws by the ſanction of religion. We ſhall find ſome (like Magno Capac and his ſiſter Caya Mama) proclaim themſelves children of God, and revealers of his will; others like Lycurgus and Numa, deliver their laws as the oracles of Heaven. True religion is emphatically ſtyled by the judicious Hooker, the root of all true virtue, and the ſtay of all well-ordered common-wealths. And even in falſe religion there are ſome true principles diſcoverable by the light of nature, which, however clouded by ſuperſtition and idolatry, are not without their deſired effect in checking the irregular paſſions of men. To the in-fluence of theſe true principles muſt be aſcribed that integrity of manners, that virtuous ſeverity, that unſhaken fortitude, and that generous love of mankind which ſhone forth even in the midſt of the darkneſs which overſpread the Heathen world.

Philoſophy, as it is connected with religion, de-ſerves to be next conſidered. The firſt philoſophers who travelled from Greece and Italy to Egypt, ſeem to have devoted their time chiefly to the ſtudy of Geometry, Aſtronomy, and Arithmetic; and it

L   muſt

muft be confeffed that Thales, Pythagoras, and their immediate fucceffors, made an aftonifhing progrefs in thofe fciences; not that they were unacquainted with the Theology of Egypt; it is well known that the latter derived from thence his favourite opinion of the tranfmigration of fouls; he likewife inculcated fome moral precepts, but thefe were expreffed in a myftical jargon, unintelligible to all except his difciples. The air of folemnity with which he delivered his doctrines, the obfcurity in which they were veiled, and the fecrecy which he enjoined to his followers, are to me arguments not fo much of the importance of the truths he revealed, as of the danger of difclofing them to vulgar ears.

At the time this great philofopher flourifhed, Italy and Greece were full of fmall governments, or rather tyrannies; in which the ufurped power of the chief magiftrate was principally employed to opprefs his fubjects.

At fuch a time Moral Philofophy, as it afcertains the relative and focial duties, is the true bafis of good laws; and above all, as it afferts the dignity of human nature, muft be grating to the ears of tyrants, and confequently dangerous to its profeffors. Yet Pythagoras had the ability to overcome every obftacle, and to reform the government of Crotona, leading the inhabitants from luxury and

libertinifm,

libertinifm, to fobriety, virtue, and the enjoyment
of equal laws. Succeeding philofophers, encouraged
by his example, applied themfelves to politics, and
by a clofe attention to the regularity, the political
œconomy, the wife laws and ftrict morals which at
that time characterifed the Egyptian government,
they feem to have acquired a juft notion of the importance of fubordination and order, and to be fully
fenfible of the advantages a fociety receives from
the united labours of every individual employed in
one common caufe. At the fame time they obferved, that the Egyptians, by carrying their love of
order and regularity too far, checked the exertions
of genius, and debafed the dignity of human nature,
by converting man into a mere machine; that from
a blind attachment to ancient cuftoms, they never
fuffered a law, however abfurd, to be abrogated, although the occafion for which it was firft enacted
had ceafed for many ages. Thefe confiderations
convinced them that their laws, though in appearance fpecious, were dictated by a real fpirit of tyranny. The Phœnicians were at that time an enlightened and commercial people; and their form
of government, which was republican, I conceive
to have been moft agreeable to the difpofition of the
Greeks, in whom a love of liberty was always a
predominant paffion. From a mixture of the Phœ-
nician and Egyptian polity, accompanied with fome
local inftitutions, the republics of Greece were

formed:

formed: from the latter they borrowed the principle and fpirit of their laws, from the former the diftribution of the legiflative and executive powers.

That quick and vivid genius for which the Greeks in all ages have been fo celebrated, was refined, not checked, by their political inftitutions; and that love of order, and attachment to ancient cuftoms, which in the Egyptian was a cold and lifelefs principle, in the Greek was fucceeded by a warm and generous patriotifm. Thofe paffions which foften without enfeebling the mind; the ties of children, kindred, and friends; accompanied with a grateful love of that country, and thofe laws to whofe protection they were indebted for fo many fignal bleffings; all thefe, ennobled by a native elevation of thought, and an enthufiaftic defire of glory, unite to form this principle, the nobleft of any which can fire the human breaft. Moral Philofophy and Legiflation were at firft joined in the characters of Lycurgus and Solon: Socrates feparated them; he occafionally exerted himfelf both in the council and in the field, to maintain the liberties of his country; yet he confined himfelf chiefly to the ftudy of Moral Philofophy, and never attempted any material reform in the ftate. The doctrines inculcated by this great philofopher, if we confider their purity and importance, are fo admirable, that we may venture to affirm, that he was acquainted with
almoft

almoſt every moral truth diſcoverable by the mere light of nature. His diſciple Plato followed his ſteps, but joined to the philoſophy of his great maſter, the Pythagorean attachment to Aſtronomy and Figures. He refined on the doctrine of the Metempſychoſis, and taught that the ſouls of vicious men, after their ſeparation from the body, were tormented with thoſe paſſions which they had improperly indulged whilſt living in union with it. He ſtrongly inculcates the · doctrine of future rewards and puniſhments; and, in a word, his writings, contain an inexhauſtible fund of good ſenſe and morality, adorned in ſome parts with fable and allegory, and in other parts refined by acute and abſtract reaſoning. It is to be lamented that he ſo frequently indulged this latter talent; for in his metaphyſical inquiries into the eſſence of the Deity, he ſometimes loſes ſight of his moral attributes. Xenophon, a diſciple of Socrates, delivered his philoſophy with more ſimplicity, and adhered with greater ſtrictneſs to the doctrines of his maſter. Euripides, though a tragic poet, deſerves a diſtinguiſhed place as a moral philoſopher. He gives us a true picture of human nature; and no writer appears to have poſſeſſed a more ſincere and unfeigned love of virtue, or to have defined the relative and ſocial duties with greater accuracy.

In

In.Ariftotle's Ethics we fee that acutenefs and penetration, that fublime and comprehenfive reach of thought; which enabled him to purfue Nature through all her deep recceffes. The juftnefs of his definitions, and his nice difcriminations of the confines of virtue and vice, ftrike even the Chriftian reader with admiration (I fpeak in general terms, for in fome parts he is doubtlefs exceptionable). In a word, we may venture to pronounce, that the Greeks in the time of Alexander the Great, far exceeded the Egyptians their mafters, or indeed any nation of antiquity, in the knowledge of moral truth ; but this knowledge though the beft that the mere light of nature could afford, falls infinitely fhort of what is revealed to us in the Gofpel. Of fome doctrines of the greateft importance, fuch as the fall and redemption of mankind, they were confeffedly ignorant. Their belief of the ftate of future rewards and punifhments was clouded by the fables of their poets and the dreams of their philofophers, and feems to have been inculcated rather as a political, than a religious truth ; that many of their moft celebrated philofophers difbelieved it, is undeniable. The method adopted by almoft all of them, of delivering two oppofite doctrines, the one calculated for the underftanding of the vulgar, and the other defigned only for thofe whofe mental powers had been improved by reflection and ftudy, fills their writings with ftrange contradictions ; and at

this

this diſtance of time we are frequently at a loſs to
diſcover what their real opinions were on the moſt
important ſubjeĉts. They are likewiſe juſtly charge-
able with making the peace and happineſs of ſociety
the ultimate end of all their philoſophy; and we
ſee them often ſacrifice morality to politics, truth
to utility. That truth is inſeparably conneĉted with
real utility, and morality with ſound politics, cannot
be denied; but to a being of ſuch limited faculties
as man, whoſe knowledge, even in what relates to
his own happineſs, is imperfeĉt and ſuperficial, caſes
muſt frequently occur, in which his duty and apparent intereſt muſt be at variance, if from an enlarged way of thinking and a native elevation of
mind, he is led to ſacrifice private conſiderations
to the good of the ſociety to which he belongs.—
Yet when the miſtaken intereſt of his country calls
upon him to violate any of the moral duties, I ſee
no principle to reſtrain him, as his views are bound-
ed by what he ſuppoſes to be the general good.
This will account for the lawleſs ambition, the in-
juſtice, and even the cruelty of ſome of the greateſt
names in antiquity, who have been at the ſame time
deſervedly admired for their humility, moderation,
juſtice, and benevolence. They were ſenſible whilſt
aĉting like private men and citizens, that a ſtriĉt
regard to morals was abſolutely neceſſary for the
exiſtence and well-being of ſociety: but when
dazzled by the ſplendour of conqueſt, or bewildered

in

in the dark and intricate mazes of policy, as they
loft fight of the utility of virtue, fo they too often
difregarded her dictates. It is remarkable that the
ancient philofophers, even whilft they taught the moft
fublime truths, fo far from exprefling any averfion
to the fuperftition and idolatry of the national religion, encouraged, both by precept and example, an
external conformity to its moft abfurd ceremonies.
But this apparent inconfiftency may be afcribed to
the fame principle, viz. a blind attachment to the
laws and conftitution of their country: they faw
the national religion fo clofely interwoven with the
ftate, that a reform of the one could not be attempted without threatening the entire fubverfion of
the other; to which I may add, that the civil magiftrate who generally prefided at their religious
ceremonies, never failed to punifh any innovation
with the greateft feverity; he permitted the philofophers to teach what doctrines they pleafed in the
fchools, becaufe he regarded their opinions in general as innocent and amufing fpeculations; but if
any of them were fuppofed to have the moft remote
tendency to leffen the reverence due to the national
religion, the propagator of fuch opinions was confidered as a criminal, and punifhable by the laws.
The prince of philofophers, Socrates himfelf, is a
melancholy example of the truth of this affertion.
The charge of Atheifm, which was brought againft
him, was too abfurd to gain credit even with the
                                              vulgar;

vulgar; his great crime feems to have been fome oblique reflections on the national religion, and the general bent of his doctrines to establish truth, whose near approach error and superstition could not bear.

It is, I believe, univerfally allowed, that the ecclefiaftical power, as feparate from, and independent on, the civil, was unknown till the eftablifhment of Chriftianity. It appears from the teftimony of Homer, Herodotus, Diodorus Siculus, Plutarch, and Plato, that among the enlightened nations of antiquity, the moft folemn rites of religion were performed by thofe who held the higheft *civil* offices. Thus religion was always under the immediate infpection of the chief magiftrate, who converted it into a mere creature of the ftate. Some of the modern Deifts are very fond of extolling the liberal and tolerating fpirit of the ancient Greeks, on the fubject of religion: what feems to have given rife to this opinion, is that intercommunity of worfhip which prevailed among all the Heathen nations; but this may be accounted for on other principles. The objects of adoration among mankind, as I have obferved before, were either the works of nature, which I term elementary, or dead men deifyed, which I call hero worfhip. In the firft cafe there could be but little diverfity of fentiment; as the objects of adoration were likewife the objects of

M

fenfe ;

sense; in the latter case, the deities were local, and tutelar, and could not suffer in their dignity, by a communication with the gods of other nations, since, by universal consent, every deity was allowed a superiority in his own country: but what principally weighed with them, was the consideration that this admission of strange gods, rather tended to confirm than lessen the authority of the national religion; since it acknowledged the principle of it to be true. But when a people appeared, who adored one God, to the exclusion of every other deity, they were regarded by the Heathen world with horror and detestation. This was the case of the Jews, whose history contains a lamentable detail of the oppressions and persecutions they suffered on account of their religion. Tacitus, a grave and impartial historian, and who, on other occasions, appears to be a man of consummate wisdom and virtue, passes over the horrid cruelties of Antiochus Epiphanes, without a single censure. The short account he gives of the Jewish nation is full of calumny and childish fable; neither does he appear to be better informed in what he says of the Christians; he expresses indeed a cool disapprobation of the cruel persecution of Nero; but that noble and virtuous indignation against tyranny and vice, which so often breaks forth in the boldest energy of expression in other parts of his history, seems on this occasion to desert him. What must we think of the prejudices of the vulgar,

when

when a mind like that of Tacitus, enlarged by learning and experience, ennobled by virtue, and refined
by humanity, fhould be thus miferably perverted:
but if any perfon can yet doubt of the intolerant
fpirit of Paganifm, let him read with an unpreju-
diced eye the perfecutions of the primitive Chrif-
tians. I am fenfible that a modern hiftorian, whofe
enmity to Chriftianity is the more dangerous, becaufe it is concealed, has endeavoured to throw a
veil over the horrors of this difgraceful part of the
Roman hiftory; but he has been fo frequently de-
tected in mifreprefenting well-known facts, that his
love for truth may be well fufpected.

The ancient Philofophers are likewife juftly re-
proached with a narrow felfifhnefs of temper; filled
with vaft ideas of their own fuperiority, they feem to
confider the generality of mankind as beneath their
notice, and unworthy the participation of thofe fublime doctrines which they communicated to their
difciples. How different this from the benevolent
fpirit of the Gofpel, which to all mankind, without
diftinction of perfons, offers the terms of life and
falvation! To conclude; the Moral Philofophy of the
Greeks, though wonderful, if we confider it as the
difcovery of mere human reafon, yet is as much inferior to the doctrines of the Chriftian religion, as
the human is inferior to the divine nature. Two
opinions have been adopted, which I hold to be

equally dangerous : one, that the Greek Philofophy is fufficient of itfelf to effect the falvation of mankind. To this I anfwer, that there are many truths not difcoverable by human reafon, in which every man is deeply interefted ; fuch, to give only one inftance, is pardon for fins on a fincere repentance; this truth without divine revelation could never have been known, yet without this who can hope for falvation! The Greek Philofophy might indeed af-certain the relative and focial duties with fome accuracy; but muft fail in its attempt to fhew the relation in which man ftood as a creature to God his Creator; befides it wanted divine authority to enforce it. On the other hand, thofe perfons are no lefs injudicious, who, becaufe they fee fome moral duties more accurately defined in the Gofpel, than in the books of Philofophers, and others en-forced, of which the Philofophers were ignorant, condemn without examination all their moral wri-tings, as contradictory to the genius and fpirit of our religion; when a moment's reflection muft teach them that without altering our nature, our Saviour could not poffibly have taught a morality wholly different from what had already been received in the world; that he confiderably improved it is ad-mitted; we will likewife add, that he enlarged our fphere of action, that he inculcated a virtue more fublime, a benevolence more extenfive, and a piety more rational and fervent; and, above all, that he

enforced

enforced his doctrines by a certain assurance of eternal happiness to the good, and everlasting torments to the wicked.

Let us then thankfully adore that God who has imparted to us such signal blessings; and as we excel the Heathens in light and knowledge, so let us endeavour to excel them in piety and virtue, and not by depending on the mere light of nature as an infallible guide—fall into what is called modern Deism, but more properly deserves the name of irreligion; or by wholly neglecting her aid, run into the opposite extreme of fanaticism, since both frequently terminate in Atheism.

Wisdom is imparted to mankind by God in different ways; some truths are discoverable by the light of nature, others by revelation. There is in the world (to use the words of the incomparable Hooker) no kind of knowledge whereby any truth is seen, but we justly account it precious, yea, that principal truth, in comparison whereof all other knowledge is vile, may receive from it some kind of light. Whether it be that Egyptian or Chaldean wisdom mathematical, wherewith Moses and Daniel were furnished; or that natural, moral, and civil wisdom, wherewith Solomon excelled all men; or that rational and oratorial wisdom of the Grecians, which the apostle St. Paul brought from Tarsus, or that Judaical which

he

he learnt fitting at the feet of Gamaliel : to detract
from the dignity whereof, were to injure God himfelf, who being that Light which none can approach
to, hath fent out thefe lights whereof we are capable,
even as fo many fparkles refembling the bright Fountain from which they rife.

NATURAL

NATURAL PHILOSOPHY.

GOD, who is the Fountain of light and know-ledge, has communicated to various parts of the creation, certain portions of his wifdom. From thefe rays of divinity, vifible in the properties of minerals and plants, the qualities of animals, and above all in the intellectual powers of man, collected and arranged by human ingenuity, every art and fcience is formed; from hence too might be traced the diftinction between fenfe and knowledge; the former of which is employed on individuals, the latter on generals. In the early ftages of fociety, before men have learned the art of reducing their ideas under general heads, we find their knowledge was very limited, although their fenfe is frequently acute and penetrating; but when their minds are improved by an intercourfe with ftrangers, or en-lightened by the fuperior talents of one of thofe benefactors to mankind, fent by God to reclaim the world from barbarifm, we fhall fee them unite in a more regular and well ordered fociety; and as the means of fubfiftence are much eafier, they will confequently have more time to devote to the culti-
vation

vation of their underſtandings: this will lead to
the invention of arts and ſciences. But when man
firſt contemplates the works of the creation, his
underſtanding will be confounded by the magnitude
of ſome objects, and diſtracted by the multitude of
others. To overcome theſe difficulties, required
the utmoſt exertions of human genius, and was at
length happily effected by the invention of geometry
and arithmetic. The former of theſe ſciences, is
unqueſtionably of Egyptian origin, and owed its
riſe to the neceſſity the Egyptians lay under, of
accurately meaſuring their lands, which were annu-
ally overflowed by the inundation of the Nile.
Theſe lands were divided into encloſures of various
figures and dimenſions, as the accidental partition
of property directed. Some were circular, others
triangular, ſquare, polygonal, &c. To facilitate
labour, as well as to indulge that curioſity and love
of knowledge, which is natural to the human mind,
the ingenuity of man was employed, in conſidering
the various properties of theſe figures, and he was
aſtoniſhed at the diſcoveries he made, which were
evergreater than his vanity could at firſt ſight imagine.
He found himſelf able not only to meaſure rocks,
mountains, and the moſt ſtupendous objects on the
ſurface of the earth, but even the whole habitable
world itſelf; nor could this ſatisfy his daring ambition, he adventured boldly through that illimitable
ſpace, in which the heavenly bodies move, marked
                                        their

their diftances, afcertained their motions, and foretold the vifible effects of their oppofitions and conjunctions. Thus far he was fuccefsful; but when he pretended to explain their fecret influence on fublunary bodies, and by that means to prognofticate future events, he fell into wild imaginations and childifh fuperftitions; and if the ftrength of the human underftanding appears in its aftronomical difcoveries, its weaknefs is in nothing more manifeft, than its aftrological dreams. Arithmetic, though probably of Egyptian invention, was chiefly cultivated by the Phenicians. This proceeded from their early addicting themfelves to trade. Situated at the extremity of the Mediterranean-Sea, they might juftly be termed a centre of union for the European and Afiatic commerce. Mount Libanus afforded them excellent materials for building their fhips; poffeffed of a limited territory, and encompaffed by warlike nations, only a fmall part of their people could be employed in agriculture. They therefore very prudently applied themfelves to naval affairs, and depending on trade for fupport, foon rofe to a degree of wealth and grandeur which aftonifhed the world. Ezekiel, in the magnificent ftyle of the prophetic writings, terms the merchants of Tyre, princes. This brave people appeared with redoubled fplendour after the deftruction of their city by Nebuchadnezzar; even furvived the dreadful cruelties of Alexander the Great, and were not finally

N   deftroyed

destroyed till invaded by the Saracens, during the reigns of their caliphs: this last overthrow they never recovered. Then, and not till then, were the prophecies of Ezekiel relating to that city, fulfilled in the utmost exteut.

Among a people, who for so many ages directed the commerce of the world, it is impossible but arithmetic in all its various branches must be perfectly understood. And the powers of numbers were soon found to be no less useful to mankind, than geometry; not only in the ordinary transactions of life, but in the investigation of sublime and speculative truths. For as there is scarcely any magnitude or distance, but what may be comprehended by geometry, so there is scarcely any multitude however great, which is beyond the reach of arithmetic. Justly therefore did the ancients term geometry and arithmetic, the wings by which men fly to heaven. Let us for a moment consider geometry as unfolding itself in mechanics, navigation, optics, geography, and astronomy. Let us trace arithmetic from its most simple form of an addition sum, to the extraction of the square and cube root; ascending still higher, let us contemplate the intricate theorems of algebra, or enter on the vast field of fluxions, and then confess, that to geometry and arithmetic we are indebted for those arts, which contribute to the comfort and ornament of life, and

thofe

thofe fciences, which by enlarging our views, make us feel the wonderful powers of the human foul, and gives us more juft and adequate ideas of the perfections of the Deity. Mankind having acquired an imperfeƈt knowledge of thefe fciences, applied themfelves with ardour to the difcovery of fpeculative and praƈtical truths; and it is reafonable to fuppofe, that fome men of a ferious turn of thought, and fuperior reach of underftanding, would devote their lives wholly to ftudy and contemplation. Such were the Egyptian priefts, fo celebrated by all antiquity for the vaft extent of their knowledge, which we are told, comprehended the liberal fciences, hieroglyphics, geography, aftronomy, natural philofophy, the difcipline of virtues and laws, the nature of the gods, the mode of worfhip by facrifices, and the whole fcience of medicine. I have already taken notice in my former differtations of their fkill in aftronomy and hieroglyphics, enlarged on their theology, and flightly touched on their morality and politics. I fhall therefore confine myfelf at prefent to their Natural Philofophy. That they were fkilful in medicine, is generally affirmed by the ancients, and the rife and progrefs of that art in Egypt has been well explained by the learned Warburton. Every prodigy and irregularity in nature, as we are informed by Strabo, was obferved by the priefts of that nation, and carefully depofited in their facred records; and Herodotus tells us, that they had more obfervations of that fort,

than

than any other nation, which they not only diligently
preferved, but frequently compared together, and
from a fimilitude of prodigies, gathered a fimilitude
of events. From this we may infer, that they had
made fome advances in Natural Philofophy; certain
it is, that not only the poets and legiflators of
Greece, but their ableft philofophers acquired the
chief of their knowledge and wifdom in Egypt.
From Egypt, Natural Philofophy found its way to
Phenicia, and was communicated by that people in
their long voyages, to every part of the known
world. Unfortunately we have no writings of the
Phenicians extant, except a fragment of Sanchoniathon preferved by Eufebius, which has occafioned
much difpute in the learned world. But the great
glory of Phenicia, according to Dr. Cudworth, was
Mofchus, or Mochus, the inventor of the Atomical Philofophy. This great man defined matter
to be extended bulk, and attributed nothing to it,
but what is included in the nature and idea of it,
viz. more or lefs magnitude, divifibility into parts,
figure, and pofition, together with motion and reft;
but fo that no body can move of itfelf, but is always
moved by fomething elfe. That there are no qualities really exifting in the bodies without, but what
are the refult or aggregates of thofe fimple elements,
and the difpofitions of the infenfible parts of bodies,
in refpeft of figure, fite, and motion; that the other
imaginary qualities of bodies, fuch as colour, tafte,

and

and fmell, are not really exifting in the bodies, but may be confidered as fancies, paffions, and fenfa- tions, occafioned by the impreffions made on our fenfes by external objects. This matter was regard- ed by Mofchus, as the fubftance from which all bodies were formed, and from the properties afcri- bed to it by the above cited definition, he thought himfelf able to account for the appearances and changes in the inanimate parts of the creation; but when he confidered the nature of the fenfitive foul of animals, and the intellectual foul of man, he found that no poffible difpofition of matter, could communicate to it a power of Loco Motion; or any imaginable combination of its properties, infpire it with any thing like thought or defign. This led him to a difcovery of another principle, diftinct from matter, which the ancient philofophers termed mind, or intellect. This opened a vaft field for the human underftanding to range in, till rifing by de- grees from the contemplation of natural objects, to the moral government of the univerfe, it formed to itfelf juft conceptions of the Deity. This Atomical Philofophy was introduced into Greece by Demo- critus, but his knowledge of it was imperfect and partial; he rejected the immaterial or active, and adopted only the material or paffive principle. From his inability to account for the formation and government of the univerfe, he found himfelf ob- liged to refer every thing to chance; neither was

he

he happier in his attempts to explain the operations of the human mind. This Philofophy, which was afterwards improved by Epicurus, and adorned by the brilliant fancy of Lucretius, abounds with ftrange abfurdities, and has a fatal tendency to Atheifm. Nothing could ever have recommended it to the world, had it not unhappily encouraged thofe vicious inclinations, which too frequently gain the afcendant in minds diffipated by trifles, and foftened by luxury. Plato is thought by many to err in the other extreme, and frequently to adopt the immaterial, to the exclufion of the material principle. But acknowledging this to be the cafe, it is the error of a great genius; nor ought we to wonder, that the human faculties, like the organs of fenfe, fhould be dazzled by an excefs of light.

Thales, who was the founder of the Ionic fchool, and who firft introduced the ftudy of Natural Philofophy into Greece, was born at Miletus in the thirty-firft Olympiad. Apuleius, fpeaking of this extraordinary man, expreffes himfelf nearly in the following manner: Of the feven wife men fo renowned in Greece, the firft rank is due to Thales; for he among the Greeks, is efteemed the firft inventor of geometry, the moft fagacious inquirer into the nature of things, and the moft fkilful obferver of the ftars; by fmall lines he difcovered the moft hidden truths, the revolutions of times, the

blowing

blowing of the winds, the meatus or fmall paffages of the ftars, the miraculous founds of thunder, the oblique courfes of the ftars, the annual returns or folftices of the fun, the fucceffive increafe and decreafe of the moon, and the obftacles which caufe an eclipfe. From this account, it is clear that the Philofophy of Thales was chiefly occupied in the contemplation of things fenfible and natural; and it is well obferved by Gale, that the Natural Philofophy of Thales, was no other than a natural hiftory of the origin of the univerfe, or in other terms, of the creation of the world, which it is imagined he received from Sanchoniathon and Mofchus. For when Philofophy began firft to take place in Greece, the grand queftion was touching the firft matter in the univerfe. For that the world had a beginning, was not queftioned till the time of Ariftotle. Thales affirmed water to be the beginning of all things, and that God out of water framed all things. This ύδωρ, or water of Thales, is confidered by the learned, as the fame with the chaos of Sanchoniathon, and from the converfion of the fpirit with the chaos, there refulted μωτ or ιλτν, which is termed matter, i. e. mud, flime, or watery mixture, which indeed was but the effect, or groffer part of that water, which Thales makes to be the material principle of all natural bodies. Thus we fee (to ufe the words of the admirable Stillingfleet) how Thales, with the Phenicians, from whom he was derived, and other

3 philofophers,

philofophers, concur with Mofes, not only in the production of the world, but in the manner of it, wherein is expreffed a fluid matter, which was the material principle. The Spirit of God moved on the face of the waters. The other philofophic opinions of Thales were, Firft, That there was one world, and that made by God the Spirit, out of the aforefaid water; and that this world, being God's workmanfhip, was exceeding beautiful, good, and perfect. Secondly, That this beauty and per- fection confifted in the admirable difpofition and harmony of its parts; in this he was followed by Pythagoras, who for this reafon termed the world κοσμος. Thirdly, Thales affirmed the world to be animated; an opinion which Plato confiderably im- proved, by fuppofing the world to be vivified by the Spirit or Providence of God. Fourthly, That night was older than the day. I fhall not at prefent enlarge on the difcoveries Thales made in aftrono- my, having already faid fufficient on that fubject, in a former differtation. Thales was fucceeded in his fchool by Anaximander, his kinfman and dif- ciple ; he differed in fome opinions from his mafter, particularly in afferting that infinity is the principle of all things. What he meant by this infinity is thus explained by Plutarch: Anaximander the Mi- lefian affirms infinite to be the firft principle, and that all things are generated out of it, and cor- rupted again into it, and therefore that infinite

worlds

worlds are thus generated and corrupted; and he gives the reafon why it is infinite, that fo there might be never any fail of generations: but in this he is miftaken, that affigning only a material caufe, he takes away the active principle of things, for Anaximander's infinite is nothing elfe but matter; but matter can produce nothing, unlefs there be alfo an active caufe. From this it appears that the Philofophy of Anaximander had an atheiftical tendency. Not that he was fo bold as to deny the exiftence of the gods; for we learn from Cicero, that Anaximander's opinion was, that the gods were native, rifing and vanifhing again in long periods of time, and that thefe gods were innumerable worlds: but how can we conceive that to be a god which is not eternal? From hence it is evident, that although Anaximander retained the names of gods, yet he denied the exiftence of a Deity. And making infinite matter to be his firft principle, he fuppofed firft the elements of earth, water, air, and fire; next the bodies of the fun, moon, and ftars; then the bodies and fouls of men, and other animals; and, laftly, innumerable or infinite worlds, as fo many fecondary and native gods to have been generated. Anaximander is faid to have made confiderable improvements in geometry, to have publifhed geographical tables, and to have been the firft of all the Greeks who found out the obliquity of the zodiac. The fucceffor of Anaximander was

O   Anaximenes,

Anaximenes, who held that air was the principle of the univerfe, of which all things were engendered, and into which they are all ultimately refolvable. That our fouls, by which we live, are air; fo fpirit and air contain in being all the world; for fpirit and air, are two names, fignifying one thing. Thus we fee that Anaximenes, although he differed from his mafter Anaximander, in making the firft matter to be air, yet agreed with him unhappily, in affign-ing only a material caufe in the univerfe, and adopting the paffive, to the exclufion of the active principle. Anaximenes was fucceeded by Anaxa-goras the Clazomenian, who was born in the firft year of the feventieth Olympiad. This great man tranflated the fchool from Afia to Athens, and had the fingular felicity of numbering among his fcho-lars, the immortal names of Pericles, Euripides, and Socrates;—impelled by an uncommon elevation of thought, he rejected the fyftems of his immediate predeceffors in the Ionic fchool, as confufed, unfa-tisfactory, and impious; and maintained, that befides the material, there was an immaterial principle, which was God. This God, as we learn from Lanctantius, he termed an infinine and felf-moving mind; and Cicero informs us, that he held this di-vine infinite mind, not enclofed in any body, to be the efficient caufe of all things. He denied that there were a multitude of unmade minds, coexifting from eternity, and confequently acknowledged one

God,

God, ruling over all. But it muſt be confeſſed, that although Anaxagoras affirmed that the world had a beginning, yet he ſeems to admit the eternity of matter, and ſuppoſed that God formed the world by his power, wiſdom, and goodneſs, from materials already exiſting, and that he rather modified and regulated, than created. This miſtake originated in extending too far that old philoſophical axiom, which ought to be received with great limitations, viz. That nothing is made out of nothing. Were I to relate all the improvements Anaxagoras made in Natural Philoſophy, my reader would probably think me tedious; I ſhall therefore only obſerve, that although his aſtronomical obſervations, ſince our late diſcoveries in that ſcience, may appear ill founded, yet they argue a wonderful reach of thought, and an uncommon force of genius. He gives on the whole a rational account of winds, thunder, earthquakes, and other phenomena in nature; and well obſerves, that the rainbow is cauſed by the refraction of the ſun's light ſtriking on a thick and watery cloud.— Having thus gone through the Ionic ſchool, from its firſt founder Thales, to Anaxagoras, who was contemporary with Socrates, I ſhall proceed to conſider the opinions of the Italic ſchool, which was founded by Pythagoras, in that part of Italy, which from the frequency of Greek colonies, was called Magna Grecia. This great philoſopher, according to the moſt received account, was born at Sidon in Phenicia, but educated

at

at Samos; it is generally allowed, that he flourished about the sixtieth Olympiad. All the writers of his life agree, that to the advantages of birth, person, and addrefs, he joined a genius vaft and fublime, and a spirit bold, daring, and unwearied in the search of truth. These happy difpofitions he did not fail to improve by study and travel.—Thus Apuleius. But the more general opinion is, that he (Pythagoras) of his own accord fought after the Egyptian fciences, and learned of the Egyptian priests, the incredible efficacy of their ceremonies, the wonderful changes of numbers, and the moft exact rules of geometry; but his mind not being fatisfied with these fciences, he went to the Chaldeans, and from them to the Brachmans and Gymnofophifts: the Chaldeans taught aftronomy, the ftated courfes of the wandering ftars, and their influence on the human conftitution. Moreover Pythagoras embraced for his mafter, Phe-recydes, a native of the ifle of Syrus, who firft rejecting the fhackles of verfe, boldly wrote Philofo-phy in profe; it is likewife affirmed, that he ftudied Natural Philofophy under Anaximander the Milefian, that he followed Epimenides of Crete, &c. From the Egyptians and Chaldeans he is faid to have learned the true folar fyftem; and from his mafter Pherecydes Syrus, to have derived his notion of the immortality of the foul. His doctrine of the metempfychofis, his ideas of the Deity, and above all his fkill in politics and legiflation, I have already

2   taken

taken notice of in a former differtation. Let us then confine ourfelves at prefent chiefly to his Phyfics, or Natural Philofophy, properly fo called. To this ftudy, Pythagoras conceived the mathematics to be preparatory, and began with teaching his fcholars arithmetic. This part of the mathematics he learned from the Phenicians, and finding it of wonderful ufe in his philofophical inquiries, he feems to have contracted for it a fuperftitious regard, and to have afcribed to it ftrange and myfterious powers: he like-wife made his fcholars apply themfelves diligently to geometry. Paffing over the numberlefs improvements he made in that fcience, I fhall take notice only of the two famous theorems which are allowed to be of his invention, viz. That every triangle is equal to two right angles, and that the fquare of the hypoteneufe of every right angled triangle, is equal to the fquare of the other two fides. Thefe two propofitions may be confidered as the bafis of trigonometry, the ex-tenfive ufe of which in practical, as well as fpecula-tive mathematics, is fo well known, that to enlarge upon it will be needlefs. Let me only obferve to thofe, who have never applied themfelves to ftudies of this fort, that the whole art of navigation is dedu-ced from thefe propofitions of Pythagoras; and that we are indebted to the labours and ingenuity of a philo-fopher who has been dead upwards of two thoufand years, for the facility with which we vifit foreign climes, and confequently for the extenfion of our commerce.

Such

Such are the advantages derived to mankind from true fcience. Natural Philofophy, or Phyfics, may be divided into the contemplative and active. Pythagoras's knowledge of the former, confifted chiefly in the hiftory of the creation, in which he does not differ materially from his great mafter Thales. The fyftems of both are conformable to the Mofaic account. Pythagoras held fire to be the principle of all things; which is thus explained by learned commentator on Plato. The element of fire is nothing elfe but a fiery fpirit, or efficacy, which is varioufly diffufed in the fymmetry of the univerfe, for the nourifhing and fomenting all things, according to their refpective natures; which vivific natural heat, Mofes calls the Spirit of God. This opinion of the efficacy or fpirituality of fire, Pythagoras probably learned from the Chaldeans. In active phyfics, or medicine, Pythagoras and his followers were well verfed; and we are told, that the chief part of their medical fkill confifted in an exact regimen or right order of diet. Certain it is that no philofopher ever inculcated more forcibly, both by precept and example, the virtue of temperance; he commanded his followers to abftain from all meats which load the ftomach, ingender humours, or inflame the blood. For the great object of Philofophy, he faid, was to preferve the health of the body and the purity of the mind. Having thus treated briefly of the Natural Philofophy of Pythagoras, it may not be improper to fay fomething

thing of his manner of philofophifing in general, which was chiefly by fymbols. This method he learned from the Egyptians, and which, in fact, is only a part of the doctrine of hieroglyphics, or rather hieroglyphic images expreffed in words. Thus a debauched worthlefs character, he defcribed by the fymbol of a coffin, which is a well-known hieroglyphic image to reprefent natural death, and, by a beautiful figure, conveys to us a true but melancholy idea of the miferable condition of a man loft to all fenfe and goodnefs. The letter Y was another favourite fymbol of Pythagoras, by which he meant to exprefs the two roads mankind enter upon, when they arrive at years of maturity; one of which leads to virtue and happinefs, the other to vice and mifery. Receive not a fwallow into thy houfe, fays Pythagoras. This fymbol Iamblichus ftrangely explains, by faying, that under it is couched a reproof againft flothful fcholars; whereas nothing is more contrary to the nature of a fwallow, than floth. The food of that bird is not to be procured without labour, confequently he is almoft always on the wing. How much more eafy and natural is it to fuppofe, that Pythagoras meant by a fwallow, a perfon of a light and talkative nature, and that it is dangerous to intruft fecrets to men of that caft. Thefe examples are fufficient to convey to my reader an idea of Pythagoras's method of philofophifing. But I cannot conclude my account of this great philofopher,

without

without giving his opinion of the providence of God, which is fo juft and rational, that I want terms to exprefs my admiration. We have need of fuch a government, fays this great man, as we ought not in any degree to contradict, which alone proceeds from the Deity, who defervedly may challenge a fovereign dominion over all; for man being fhamefully variable and fickle in his appetites and paffions, needs fuch a government, from which proceeds moderation and order: to this he adds, that good men are the peculiar care of heaven. Pythagoras was fucceeded in his fchool by his wife Theano, a woman of extraordinary genius, and his fons Telaugus and Menexarchus. Among his difciples, O-cellus, Architas, Philolaus, and Parmenides, are moft celebrated. From the two former, particularly from Ocellus, Ariftotle is thought to have borrowed much of his logic and metaphyfics. Of Parmenides they tell an idle ftory of his fpending eighteen years in a rock, feeding his mind all that time with logic, as if the only way to become a great Philofopher, was to commence enthufiaft and madman. Philolaus is chiefly known by the value Plato fet on his books, which he purchafed at an incredible price. In fpeaking of the Pythagorean philofophers, I ought not to omit Epicharmus and Timeus, to whofe metaphyfical writings on being, and ideas, it is fuppofed Plato was not a little indebted. Thus have we traced Natural Philofophy from Egypt and Phenicia, where

fhe

fhe fpent her infancy, beheld her gradually unfold
her charms during her abode in the Ionic and Italic
fchools, and we fhall now fee her in the hands of
Plato and Ariftotle, fhine forth in her full blaze of
beauty. Plato was born at Athens, or as fome fay,
in the ifland of Egina, the firft year of the eighty-
eighth Olympiad. His defcent was noble; for he
reckoned among his anceftors, Codrus, the laft king
of Athens, fo celebrated for his heroic virtues, and
moft glorious death. We are told, that whilft he
was yet an infant, and lay faft afleep in a thicket of
myrtles on mount Hymettus, a fwarm of bees fixed
on his mouth, and made an honeycomb. This was
confidered as a prefage of his future eloquence. Other
ftories of the fame nature are related—the invention
of men, who know not how to exprefs, without the
aid of fiction, their admiration of a genius fo vaft and
tranfcendant. In his youth he is faid to have compofed an epic poem; but on a comparifon with the Iliad
of Homer, finding it much inferior, he committed it
to the flames, and from that time applied himfelf
wholly to the ftudy of Philofophy. As Socrates was
his mafter in moral, fo Pythagoras feems to have been
his guide in Natural Philofophy. The writers of his
life agree, that he travelled into that part of Italy
where Pythagoras taught, and that he attended the lec-
tures of Architas and Euritus, and was a great admirer
of Timeus the Locrian. From Italy he directed his
courfe to Egypt, and was accompanied in his voyage

P   by

by Euripides. His object in this voyage, as we are
informed by Cicero, was to inftruct himfelf in the
celeftial fpeculations of the Barbarians; and during
his thirteen years refidence in that country, he no
doubt acquired a knowledge of their moft obfcure
and myfterious doctrines. Philofophy, in its moft
extenfive fenfe, may be confidered as either theore-
tical or practical. The object of the former is the
difcovery of truth, the object of the latter the practice of virtue. Phyfics, and thofe parts of meta-
phfics, which are not immediately connected with
theology, belong to the former. The latter includes
ethics, œconomics, politics, and theology. As the Ionic and Italic Philofophers applied themfelves chiefly
to the theoretic, Socrates devoted himfelf wholly to
the practical; but Plato, who afpired to the character of a complete philofopher, was determined to
unite in his own perfon, the moft diligent inquiry
into the fecrets of nature, to the moft fublime fpeculations of theology, and to lay down the beft rules
for the conduct of life, drawn from accurate obfervations on the nature of man, his propenfities
and paffions, and the different relations in which
he ftands to God, his country, family, and friends.
Such was the glorious ambition of this renowned
philofopher, which was crowned with the fuccefs
it deferved. But as the fubject of this differtation,
confines me chiefly to Phyfics, or Natural Philofophy, I muft either wholly omit, or but flightly touch

on

on the moſt ſublime and important of his doctrines.
Let us at preſent conſider his opinions relating to
the origin of the univerſe; and firſt, he held that
the world had a beginning, and that it was created
by God according to the exemplar and idea pre-
exiſting in the Divine Mind. This exemplar and
idea, he ſometimes terms the intelligible, in contra-
diſtinction to the viſible and created world; by
which he meant that the world was framed, not for-
tuitouſly or by chance, but according to the dictates
of the moſt perfect wiſdom. That as an architect in
building a palace or a temple, acts by deſign, and
forms it after an image or idea preconceived in his
mind; ſo this moſt beautiful temple of the world,
was created by God conformable to his divine ideas,
of which it was an imitation; and therefore God is
ſaid by Plato to have adorned, ordered, figured,
conſtituted, and framed all things. The general
ingredients which enter into the compoſition of all
bodies, according to this great philoſopher, are the
four elements, fire, water, earth, air; but yet theſe
elements are not, properly ſpeaking, the firſt matter,
which he terms chaos, or υλη, and thus defines it:
The genus out of which every thing is compoſed;
and he ſays it is neither fire, nor water, nor earth,
nor air, but the common mother and nurſe of all
theſe; that it is a kind of anomalous thing, not
clothed with eſſence, yea little better than nothing;
yet the common ſubject, out of which all things are

P 2   formed.

formed. My reader will doubtlefs be ftruck with the
refemblance this firft matter of Plato's bears to the
univerfe, as defcribed by Mofes, before it was animated by the Spirit of God. And the earth was
without form, and void, and darknefs was upon
the face of the deep. This darknefs is the fame as
Plato's Erebus, which not only the philofophers, but
the moft ancient poets make to be the parent of all
things. Plato thus expounds the operations of
the Divine Mind in the formation of the univerfe;
the matter of things, fays he, being fubftracted, the
mind of the Divine Opificer, by a prudent kind of
perfuafion, compelled the fame which was dark,
fluid, and unformed, to pafs into light, order, &c.
That this prudent kind of perfuafion of Plato, is the
fame as the fiat of Mofes, muft be evident to the
moft fuperficial reader. Secondly, The body of the
univerfe, which he terms vifible and tangible, he
makes, as I obferved before, to confift of four elements, fire, water, earth, and air, conjoined together by a friendly proportion and harmony. Of
thefe, he fays, earth is the moft ponderous and
impenetrable ; fire, by its tenuity, penetrates
every thing; air every thing but fire; water penetrates the earth, by which means all things being
filled, there is no vacuum. Of thefe elements, fays
Plato, God compofed the world, which is tangible,
by reafon of earth, and vifible by fire; which two
extremes are joined together by air and water, with

proportion,

proportion, that moſt excellent bond. For fire, from its penetrating nature, renders all things viſible, and nothing is tangible, but what has a ſolid baſis; now nothing is ſolid but what partakes of the earth. From this friendly junction of the elements, there reſulted beauty, harmony, and perfection; and God ſurveying the works of the creation, according to Plato, rejoiced, or in the more energetic language of Moſes, ſaw that they were good, i. e. fitted for the ends for which they were deſigned: beſides the beauty, harmony, and perfection above mentioned, Plato aſcribes to the univerſe ſeveral other qualities or affections, ſuch as generation, which he defines to be a motion to eſſence, mobility, figure, colour, &c. By the ſoul of the univerſe, I am of opinion, that he ſometimes means that providential care with which God preſerves and governs all things; at other times, only thoſe vital energies, communicated by God to the various parts of the creation, and by which they all regularly tend to their appointed end. Theſe energies have been termed by ſome philoſophers, Plaſtic Nature, or the divine art embodied. Plato was of opinion that the heavenly bodies were of an igneous and fiery nature; that the moſt glorious of all beyond compariſon was the ſun, whoſe rays illumined all things; that of the ſtars, the greater part were fixed, ſeven only being erratic; that the moon performed her revolution in twenty-nine days and a half; that the ſun paſſed through the ſigns of

the

the zodiac, and completed the feafons in a year: of the other erratic ftars, each had its particular revolution. The fentiments of this great philofo- pher on the ordinary phenomena in the lower world, fuch as gufts of wind, rain, thunder, &c. are not accurately known, but we have reafon to believe they were not very different from what were taught in the Ionic and Italic fchools before his time. Animals and plants, Plato feems to have ftudied very attentively, and by an invefligation of their properties, confiderably to have improved the fcience of medi- cine.   Let us before we take our leave of Plato, fee what are his fentiments on man, who unquefti- onably is the nobleft animal of the creation; and firft, this great philofopher tells us, nearly in the words of Mofes, that man is a kind of imitation of God, and his mafter-piece; that he confifts of foul and body, that the foul is ingenerable and immortal, and as to its capacity infinite, never fatisfied, but with the firft truth and chiefeft good; and it becomes the body to ferve, but the foul to rule, becaufe it is moft like to the divine, immortal, intelligible, moft uni- form, and perfect being; that truth is the proper object of the mind, which he terms its life and food. Wifdom he defines to be a knowledge of beings eternal; intelligence, a knowledge of firft principles; fcience, a demonftrative knowledge; opinion, he fays, is fomething that partakes of fcience and ig- norance; art, an imitation of nature, &c.   For the

body

body it is as neceffary to preferve it in health and
vigour, as to improve the mind by knowledge; and
Plato gives us many admirable rules for the confer-
vation of health, and the cure of difeafes. Like
Pythagoras, he held geometry and arithmetic, to be
fciences preparatory to the ftudy of Natural Philofophy. I fhall conclude my account of this great
philofopher, with the obfervation of Ludovicas Vives:
That there are three things which gained not only
Greece, but the whole world to Plato, viz. his integrity of life, his holy precepts, and his eloquence.
The moft renowned of all Plato's difciples, was
Ariftotle, a man, who, with incredible acutenefs, pe-
netrated into the moft fecret receffes of nature;
whofe genius, vaft and capacious, comprehended
the whole material and immaterial world; and whofe
difcriminating judgment could clearly arrange, and
accurately define the moft complex operations of the
human mind. He differed not lefs from his great
mafter in the ftriking features of his character, than
in his method of treating philofophical fubjects.
The ftyle of Plato is figurative and poetical; we fee
an artful arrangement of periods, and ftudied harmony of cadence; and frequently on the moft abftract fubjects, he addreffes himfelf to the reader's
imagination, and clothes his fublime ideas in the
thin and tranfparent robes of fable and allegory.
On the other hand, Ariftotle fpeaks only to the
underftanding; relying on the force and ftrength of

his

his reafoning, he rejects all extraneous ornaments, and delivers himfelf with a pregnant brevity; not lefs frugal of his words, than liberal of his fenfe. From their different characters we may likewife account for the different genius of their Philofophy. Plato, whofe imagination was luxuriant, and whofe feelings were acute, was fenfibly alive to religious impref-fions, and his writings abound with the moft fublime ideas of the Deity, his power, wifdom, and good-nefs, manifefted in the creation and prefervation of all things, and the moft eloquent and perfuafive ex-hortations to a life of piety and virtue, from the powerful motives of grateful love and reverential awe. But in Ariftotle, judgment was predominant; and he feems not to have poffeffed any great fhare of imagination or fenfibility. Although he was led by his underftanding to acknowledge a firft caufe, which was God, to whom he afcribes the ufual attributes; yet on two fubjects, of all others, the moft important to mankind, viz. The providence of God in the go-vernment of the world, and the immortality of the foul, he expreffes himfelf with a degree of doubt and uncertainty. This fcepticifm proceeded from the rule he had laid down, not to believe any thing which he could not bring to the level of his under-ftanding. It muft be confeffed that his writings contain many excellent doctrines, viz. That nature is the inftrument of the Deity, acting not according to the necefflity of material motions, but for ends and
purpofes,

purpofes, though unknown to itfelf; that man, in the moſt extenſive ſenſe of the word, is a free agent, and that morality is natural to him: this he admirably explains in his ethics and politics. In a word, Ariſtotle writes, as if he were addreſſing himſelf to a mere intelligence. Plato conſiders man as a compound creature, and at the ſame time that he informs his underſtanding, he endeavours to ſtrike his imagination, and move his paſſions. Having thus given a comparative view of the merits of theſe two great philoſophers, I ſhall proceed to conſider Ariſtotle's opinion touching the origin of the univerſe; and firſt, he held in a limited ſenſe, the eternity of matter. This notion he adopted, becauſe he found difficulties in conceiving a creation out of nothing. He ſeems in his idea of the firſt matter, to follow the opinion of Plato; for he ſtyles it, unformed, indeterminate, indigeſtive, a mere paſſive power, capable of any form ; and ſays, that there are three principles of nature, privation, form, and matter, which laſt is the common ſubjeЄt of both. The exemplars and divine ideas of Plato, Ariſtotle rejeЄted as unintelligible; for the reſt, in his Phyſics, he appears to have adopted the doЄtrines of his maſter Plato, though he expreſſes himſelf in different terms; and it muſt be confeſſed, that on many ſubjeЄts he explains his meaning with much greater accuracy. In the ſcience of meteorology he far exceeded him ; and in his hiſtory of animals, he ſhews ſuch a knowledge of their

Q   variou̇s

various natures, as could not poffibly be acquired
by any fingle man, unlefs affifted by the bounty of
an Alexander, who ordered animals to be brought
from different parts of the world for his infpection.
Logic, or the art of arranging our ideas, is poffeffed
in a certain degree by all mankind; for without it
no difcourfe could be held: but how imperfect this
art is in uncultivated minds, is evident from the confufed perceptions of favages, and the ftrange junction of diffimilar ideas, fo obfervable in the conver-
fation of children. Let us trace the progrefs of this
art : as foon as mankind begin to exert their rational
faculties, they obferve certain characteriftic differ-
ences, which diftinguifh the animal from the vegetable, and the vegetable from the mineral world.
Thus general ideas are formed, which may be confidered as the bafis of knowledge; afterwards, from
a more accurate furvey of nature, they difcover that
thefe general ideas of animals, vegetables, and minerals, may be fubdivided into an infinite number of
fpecies, agreeing in fome common qualities, which
mark the genus, and differing in others, which diftinguifh the fpecies: thus, by claffing every individual
under its proper genus and fpecies, men learn to think
and fpeak with accuracy; but before this can be
done, the human mind muft have made great advances in fcience; for in the fcale of nature, we
find one fpecies difcriminated from another, by fuch
nice diftinctions, as to efcape all but the philofophic

eye: to which I may add, that the number is fo
infinite, as to exceed the comprehenfion of the moft
enlarged underflanding, fo that our knowledge of
the works of nature, muft be always imperfeƐt. This
method of arrangement, which was at firft employed
on thofe ideas, which are derived from fenfible objeƐts, was afterwards applied to abftraƐt and metaphyfical conceptions. Zeno is faid to have firft given
to logic a fcientific form; but the improvements it
afterwards received from Ariftotle were fo great, as
to eclipfe the glory of all who went before him.
This great man, under ten general heads, fo well
known by the name of the Ten Predicaments, included every difference by which one individual is
diftinguifhed from another; and it is not eafy to
conceive a greater effort of the human underflanding,
than thus to reduce the infinite variety of nature,
within fo fmall a compafs. The fyllogifm is un-
queftionably of Ariftotle's invention; for although
in Plato and other writers who preceded him, we
frequently fee a method of ratiocination, yet we have
nothing like a fyllogiftic or artificial arrangement of
argument. To conclude, in the exaƐnefs of his
definitions and divifions, and in the clearnefs of his
demonftrations, Ariftotle not only excelled all the
writers who preceded him, but to this day remains
unequalled; and one may venture to pronounce,
that logic and metaphyfics, fince his time, have received no real improvement. In Natural Philofophy,

it

it muſt be confeſſed, that the Greeks in the age o
Alexander the Great, were much inferior to th
moderns; and I cannot finiſh theſe diſſertation
better, than by obſerving, that in thoſe arts an
ſciences which depend on elegance of taſte, ſpright
lineſs of fancy, and vigour of genius, the Greek
were our ſuperiors; and the only advantage w
have over them, is in thoſe uſeful arts and curiou
inveſtigations, in which labour is exerted rathe
than genius, and which cannot be brought to per
fection, but by the ſucceſſive induſtry and experienc
of many ages.

F I N I S.